Also by Beth Lindsay Templeton

Loving Our Neighbor:
A Thoughtful Approach to Helping People in Poverty

Understanding Poverty in the Classroom:
Changing Perceptions for Student Success

Angelika's Journal:
What You Can Do about Poverty and Homelessness

A Coat Named Mr. Spot

Conversations on the Porch:
Ancient Voices—Contemporary Wisdom

More Conversations on the Porch:
Ancient Voices—Contemporary Wisdom

Refrigerator Prayers for Ordinary People

The Christmas Strawberry…and Other Stories

Uncharted Journey

On the Challenges of
Getting Older and Other Transitions

Beth Lindsay Templeton

FpS

Greenville, S.C.

Uncharted Journey

On the Challenges of
Getting Older and Other Transitions of Life

Published by:

FpS

1175 Woods Crossing Rd., #5
Greenville, S.C. 29607
864-675-0540
www.fiction-addiction.com

ISBN: 978-1-945338-96-0

Cover & Book Design by Vally Sharpe
Author Photograph © 2017 Jim Banks

Printed in the United States of America.

In memory of my husband
Jim Banks

Acknowledgments

I am very grateful to all the authors listed in the Bibliography who fed my hungry soul as I began naming and claiming my own uncharted journey. Their words gave me encouragement, insight, and strength as I continued to read and learn.

The various groups of women who have allowed me to try out my ideas, struggles, and questions with them gave me courage and a sense of support. Special thanks to Becky, Judy, Carol Ann, Nancy, Frances, Biff, Susan M., and Susan S. for helping me begin and continuing to walk with me.

I am grateful to my parents, Dorcas and Denton Lindsay who, having been married now seventy-one years, are guideposts to my own uncharted journey. They and their friends at the Foothills, South Carolina, Presbyterian Communities demonstrate that life is indeed a journey and can be fulfilling even into one's nineties and beyond.

A big thanks goes to my editor, Vally Sharpe, who helps me say what I really want to say.

And none of my work would be possible without the support of my husband, Jim Banks. He provides me emotional space to explore and be creative as well as serves delicious meals to enrich my wellbeing.

I am a woman truly blessed!

Preface

To live until I die. That is my hope and dream. However, changes in life can make that desire unattainable.

There are many kinds of transitions in life: going off to school, getting a job, changing jobs, getting married, getting divorced, having children, saying goodbye as children leave home, moving, losing friends and family members, retiring, having grandchildren, losing one's health, even getting a new car or phone. All involve loss, letting go, and growth. The transition that motivated my own quest on the uncharted journey was when I left fulltime employment to begin my own company. I was also getting closer to eligibility for Medicare and Social Security!

Not health issues, not financial issues, but emotional and spiritual issues challenged my equilibrium. I felt that I was on an uncharted journey. I suppose that all of life is uncharted but moving into the years of "maturity" seemed less guided, with more unknowns.

Friends and family members had died, my job had changed, a few relationships were unstable, and the face in the mirror was no longer the face I expected to see. I realized that I was beginning yet another transition in life, an uncharted journey of getting older.

I could see what might be in store for me. My parents lived in a retirement center with multi-levels of care. I saw what life looked like there as their friends' health deteriorated. People with whom they spent time eventually moved away to be closer to family, transitioned to skilled care or the memory unit, or died. My parents began to lose their hearing, their eyesight, and their mobility was compromised. Even their attitudes changed in both positive and negative ways. What was once important was no longer and things that previously had little significance became front page news.

I struggled to figure out what was next. The circle of my friends whom I normally would have talked with had gotten significantly smaller because five of my close friends had died, before their time, in their fifties or early sixties. Two close extended family members simply dropped dead without warning. I wondered about who would be with me as I aged since it seemed that my closest confidants were gone.

I realized that some of my career dreams needed to be redefined. As a female minister for over thirty years, I had often been the first woman to preach in a congregation. I never was an installed pastor in a church and yet carved out a meaningful ministry working in a nonprofit organization working with and advocating for people who lived in poverty. I described myself as a "freelance" Presbyterian minister, filling in at churches when needed: ministers on sabbatical, congregations between installed pastors, churches in conflict. Now I witnessed younger women being called as senior pastors of large congregations. I felt both proud that women had come so far in ministry and also regretted that I was too old for that now to happen for me.

My children were grown with families of their own. They lived away and so I was not an integral part of their lives. We enjoyed our times together, but I did not feel essential to their wellbeing as I once had. My husband was dealing with his own feelings of changing body, health fears, and questions of what's next and does anyone care? And I would soon be drawing Social Security and qualify for Medicare.

I believe that when the student is ready, the teacher appears. Books have always been my friends and keys to broader understanding. I looked on my bookshelves and found, to my great surprise, *Aging* by Henri Nouwen and Walter J. Gaffney. Various books that had been in my library—many unread—jumped out at me. An acquaintance of mine, Jack Hansen, had co-authored with Jerry Haas a book on retirement. I wondered how I could get a copy of Jack's book and within days, Jack appeared in a workshop I was leading about poverty. I asked him about his book. By the end of the next week, I had a copy of *Shaping a Life of Significance for Retirement*.

I became convinced that I was learning some great information I wanted to share. I met a friend for coffee and began talking about what I was learning. I said that I needed a group to share my insights with. She said, "You need a group. I'll get you a group." We began meeting once a month in her home with a group of her friends, who are now my friends. We talked about situations that we face in our lives. We experienced safety in our sharing, laughter in our tales, comfort in our deepening trust, and relief that we have companions on this uncharted journey. From these conversations came more opportunities for sharing: other groups who met with me for a time, women's retreats, as well as my own deepening understanding of loss, letting go, and growth. Even now, I continue to read and grow through my reading, personal meditation, and conversations with friends, my husband, and my parents.

One of the amazing successes of my time with the women's groups is the quote box. As a long collector of quotes, I gathered quotes from the many books that I was reading. I put each of the quotes on a slip of paper and then put the quotes into a purple velvet box. At the end of each meeting, I passed around the box and each woman chose a quote. She knew that this may be the quote that the Spirit wanted her to have that day, even if at first the quote did not resonate with her. She could always put the quote back and pick another one. We were constantly amazed at how on point the quotes were. A woman may have shared a poignant incident or insight and the quote reinforced her or pushed just a little bit more for her growth. The affirmations of the quotes made us all realize that what we were doing was significant for each of us.

Each letter in this book begins with one of those quotes. I expect the Spirit of Truth and Insight to continue to move through the words of these writers.

I invite you to enter this time of discerning what's on your uncharted journey. As you read these letters, keep in mind this story shared by Parker Palmer in his book, *A Hidden Wholeness*:

> "The soul is like a wild animal...the soul is tough, resilient, resourceful, savvy, and self-sufficient: it knows how to survive in hard places. ... Yet, despite its toughness, the soul is also shy. Just like a wild animal, it seeks safety in the dense underbrush, especially when other people are around. If we want to see a wild animal, we know that the last thing we should do is go crashing through the woods yelling for

it to come out. But if we will walk quietly into the woods, sit patiently at the base of a tree, breathe with the earth, and fade into our surroundings, the wild creature we seek might put in an appearance. We may see it only briefly and only out of the corner of an eye—but the sight is a gift we will always treasure as an end in itself."*

Give yourself permission to let your soul...your spirit... your very self...peek out and learn what your next step may be on your uncharted journey. Let's discover ways to live fully until we die!

Beth Templeton
January, 2018

*Parker J. Palmer. *A Hidden Wholeness: The Journey Toward an Undivided Life.* Jossey-Bass, 2004. *Used with permission.*

Uncharted Journey

On the Challenges of
Getting Older and Other Transitions

1

"Aging is the turning of the wheel, the gradual fulfillment of the life cycle in which receiving matures in giving and living makes dying worthwhile. Aging does not need to be hidden or denied, but can be understood, affirmed, and experienced as a process of growth by which the mystery of life is slowly revealed to us."

— *Henri Nouwen and Walter Gaffney* —

Dear One,

One of the transitions of life that affects everyone when they are blessed to live so long is the transition of aging. This process of aging is full of the challenges of gifts of loss, letting go, and growth.

People handle aging in different ways. The differences may be based on their personalities, their circumstances at a particular time, their health, their support systems, and a variety of other factors. Some believe that life is linear, that one thing leads to another and then to another. If today is good, then tomorrow will be better. If they were successful in their career, they will be successful in their retirement. If they've always managed everything around them, they will continue to do so even now. They forget that the term life "cycle" was coined for a reason.

Life is circular or even a spiral but certainly not a straight line. Things can be going well one day and not so good the next. You may receive a disturbing phone call from a friend who has just been given a scary health diagnosis. You may have been notified that the funds you were counting on for retirement are not as plentiful as you thought. The preacher may have delivered a sermon that upset you. You just realized that you have not heard from your children or grandchildren in quite a while. Anything can make the pleasantness of just a few hours ago disappear.

On the other hand, tomorrow may be even better than today. A high school friend you lost contact with responded to something you posted on Facebook. The fig tree in your yard finally put on fruit after just sitting there for several years. You found shoes that make your feet feel better. You figured out how to fix the problem with your computer...all by yourself! You realized that you no longer care that your body looks like the age you are rather than how it did when you were twenty-five.

Life goes around and around. Lessons repeat themselves. The chance to forgive someone or to be forgiven does not happen just one time. Opportunities cycle again to repair the damage you did to a relationship. When you messed up you learned a lesson so that the next time you could handle it better.

The moment you erupted from your mother's womb, you began the process of living and dying. Life and death are interchangeable, as much as you'd like to deny that reality. Living leads to dying and, hopefully, the awareness of your death approaching encourages you to find ways to live until that moment.

Some people choose to live a living death. They close their internal house months or years before they have to move out of their bodies. They live with their inner life "furniture" draped with sheets so they miss the beautiful print on the living room chair. They refuse to pull out and dust off the treasures they have stored up in their memories so things begin to get moldy. They withdraw from friends because they know their friends will leave at some point or that they will leave the friends. Since it's going to happen anyway, why invest the time and effort to keep in touch, to share and laugh and cry together?

Grab onto the cycle of life and death. Ride that merry-go-round for all it's worth. Try out the lion, the horse, the elephant, and the tiger on the ride. See which animal on the merry-go-round gives you the most pleasure. When that ride no longer sustains your spirit, look around and see what else life is offering. Maybe swan boats on the lake? Maybe a roller coaster? Maybe a peep show? Why not?

The cycle goes around and around. Life, death, life, death, life, death. This is your reality. Affirm the mystery of your life. Embrace the opportunities that come to you in whatever form they come. You're incapacitated? Welcome your caregivers and nurture their souls. You're a bit tired of living alone and a new love enters your life? Who cares what anyone else thinks. What do you want to do?

You still have breath in your body. Wrap your arms around yourself and say, "I love me! I am a person full of mystery and vitality. I will live fully as long as I have breath. My death is a part of the wonder of my life and I will live fully until that last moment."

Don't want to do that? Okay. You choose how you will transition through the loss, letting go, and growth of this transition. You are a wonderful person. You will know what is right for you...if you will listen to that secret guide that is in you. Know that I wish you well on this uncharted journey.

With Love,
Your Secret Admirer

2

"This is why being broken is so beautiful: being broken means you have cracks for love and light to shine through, gaps for the Godiverse to burrow and bloom, space to move from the person you were to the person you will become. Being broken means healing can find you and hope can gush forth like a geyser, flooding every part of you, until you can see why the Breaking was necessary in the first place; to give birth to you."

— *Reba Riley* —

Dear One,

You are screaming inside your body. You are weeping rivers of tears. You are angry. You are dismayed.

Something has happened that you were not counting on. Perhaps your doctor told you that you will never be free of that stabbing pain in your back. Maybe you've been dismissed after years of loyal service to your company. Or your spouse has announced that your marriage is over. Or you've just learned that the money you saved for retirement is inadequate.

Your child's life is topsy-turvy in ways that you don't understand. You can't find your car keys and you're certain you're losing your mind…really. Your mom is going to have to move into an Alzheimer's unit and you have no idea how to handle that. The anniversary of your sibling's death is coming up.

Maybe what hurts so bad seems insignificant to anyone but you. The person who has done your hair for years is retiring. You've lost the ring that your grandmother, long gone, gave you. Your favorite television show got cancelled. The minister who, for many years, has walked with you on your life journey is moving to the other side of the country.

Maybe your sense of brokenness has nothing to do with anything external. You've lost your zip for life. You feel broken inside. You can't even explain why you feel this way. Something has shifted and you're not comfortable with the space that now seems like a huge chasm in your spirit. You feel...what? Can you even feel anything? Maybe not. Everything has shifted for the moment and you feel...broken.

I know that this is hard to believe at the moment but that feeling of brokenness can be a gift to you. I know, I know. The thought that brokenness could be a gift is hard for you to conceive of right now. So, go for a walk, take a hot shower, listen to some music, or drink a glass of water. Be kind to yourself.

You may be tempted to add feelings of disdain to your already wounded spirit. You may be thinking that if you were just stronger, if only you weren't so sensitive, if only you didn't have so much on you right now, if only you felt better, if only...then you could handle what is going on in your life right now. Stop the "if-only" game right now. You know IF you could, you would.

Above all, be gentle with yourself. Allow yourself to feel broken. Some people believe that if you say "ouch, ouch, ouch" loud enough when you get a paper cut on your finger that the cut will heal quicker. When you acknowledge the pain, you seem to release the body's healing power a bit sooner. The point is... you're not alone.

You may find it helpful to remember a favorite childhood toy that got broken. What did you do? Sob? Scream? Blame someone? Did you bury it—give it a decent "funeral"? You can still remember that toy and the events that rendered it useless as a play thing. Would you play with it today if it were still available? Do you still need it in your life? Or would you put it on a shelf and pull it out only at certain times. Maybe when you feel…broken?

You don't need that toy in your life anymore. You have grown beyond it. Other toys probably replaced it in your hours of play and pretend. You still remember it, but it is no longer part of you. It's gone and you're still okay.

That's the way it is with broken places in your life. The brokenness is part of clearing space for something new to sprout up. Because something is broken, you will grow—I repeat, you *will*—if you allow for the possibility. You will move to giving that part of life that's hurting so badly a "decent funeral."

I know that may be hard to believe. The sorrow you felt when you found the broken favorite toy was real and intense. But it passed. Some people say that their favorite words in all of English are: "This too shall pass."

In the brokenness, something wonderful can be happening. You may not see if for a while, maybe a long while. But something is struggling to grow out of the broken ground of your life.

Have you ever seen a meadow a year or so after a wild fire ravaged it? It is a glorious sight. The fire created openness so the sun could flood the field. The ash from the fire, the rot from the fallen trees, and vegetation created a rich bed of soil for glorious wildflowers to grow. Just imagine a field covered with red, blue, yellow, purple, orange, and white flowers. You can hardly walk without stepping on a magnificent gift from the creator God. Without the devastation of the fire and scorched earth, the flowers would not have grown.

That can happen to you. Sit, be easy with yourself. Know that from your brokenness, something new will sprout up. The new growth may be very tentative at first. It may not look anything like what came before. On the other hand, it may resemble what was broken…and yet, it will be different in its own beautiful way.

If you've been holding your breath in your pain, you will discover that you begin to breathe easily again. Not all at once. You may still struggle to get a fully deep breath, but you will notice that your chest is filling up a bit more. You will be able to forget about your brokenness for longer periods of time. You will!

Being dismissed from that job will clear your calendar for other things you may be interested in. You'll reevaluate your financial situation and learn what your next steps might need to be. Do you need to find another job? This may turn out to be the opportunity of a lifetime, something you would never have considered without being broken out of your old shell. Maybe you'll reevaluate your spending patterns and find more free events in your community or discover the joy of treasure hunting in the local charity shops.

If your woundedness is from a broken marriage, that will be painful. After a time, if you allow yourself to be open to new growth, you will discover new ways of loving. You may finally fall in love with yourself! You can make decisions on your own without needing to consult anyone else. You can arrange the furniture exactly as you choose. You can get rid of that ugly chair, those nasty clothes left lying around, and the toothpaste tops on the edge of the bathroom sink.

Slowly, slowly, you will begin to poke your little green-sprout-head up out of the ground, look around, and decide that the risk of continuing to push up toward the light is worth the struggle. You will notice on your little green stem that strange things seem to be showing themselves.

Leaves! Ah, leaves. Leaves help bring you good health and strength. And they make you prettier.

And then, what's this? Oh my, there's a bumpy thing getting bigger and bigger. It's a bud. Soon you are amazed that now there's a gorgeous flower that's part of you. The most beautiful flower that's ever been and it's you!

Someone admires your flower, picks it, and you feel a bit wounded. The cycle begins again. That's life.

Brokenness makes room for new growth which, at its time of maturity, breaks again. and the cycle goes on and on. Each time the break-growth-rebirth cycle completes itself, you become more and more yourself.

You just can't see it yet, but one day you will look back and thank God for the wound. Without it, you would not be the wonderful person you are today.

With love,
Your Secret Admirer

3

"There are only two ways to live your life. One is as though nothing is a miracle. The other is as though everything is a miracle."

— *Albert Einstein* —

Dear One,

As I sit writing my letter to you, I look out my window and see grass beginning to turn green in the spring sunshine. A few raindrops from last night's shower shimmer on the still leafless branches of the tree, a bird sings lustily—looking for its mate—and life is good.

It's hard to imagine that Albert Einstein, developer of the general theory of relativity (which led to a lot of what the science of modern physics is built upon), actually said what is shared above. But he was right—we have a choice as to which way we look at the world and how we will live our lives. There are moments when nothing about life seems a miracle. Other times shout out loud with glee that life is nothing *but* a miracle.

This is a time in your life when you can choose with more thought, more abandon, more deliberation, more intentionality, and more openness how you want to live…as if everything is a miracle or nothing—absolutely nothing—is. You might think that choosing one side of this either-or question is easy. Or maybe you think it is extremely difficult. *Hmm…*that's a conundrum.

How do you define miracle? As God intervening against the laws of nature? The gospel writers in the New Testament of the Christian Bible reported that Jesus walked on water, fed thousands with a few fish and loaves bread, and brought people back to life.

Are there other thoughts that come to mind about what a miracle is? Maybe it's a story you heard along the way.

Do you think of miracles as something that is always good, positive, and fabulous? Are they like living in wonderland? Is believing in miracles like going through life with a magic wand?

Let's look more closely at this conundrum.

Imagine that nothing is a miracle. Would you have to give up anything by believing that? Would you lose a belief that is significant to you if you were to decide that there is nothing transcendent about life? What would it feel like to believe there is no God, no universal principle, no chi?

Without miracles, everything we see, hear, smell, taste, and feel is just that…only what we see, hear, smell, taste, and feel. There is nothing more or less about anything. An apple is simply an apple. There is nothing special about it. The apple appears in the grocery store, you buy it, you eat it.

When you get sick, you recover because of sufficient medical care, appropriate medications, and rest. No miracle there.

You know that life is not all miracles. People don't have magic wands. Bad things happen. You can name a whole list of bad things right now. You do not have evidence that there is anything beyond your limited reality. After all, if there is a God, if there are such things as miracles, how could the ground shake and heave up, killing hundreds, if not thousands, of people and destroying property? If everything is a miracle, how do you explain car wrecks, floods, terminal illness, and politicians?

Living without the possibility of miracles means that everything is rational, of the mind. If you cannot conceive it, it does not exist for you. But even Albert Einstein says that we can't have it both ways. It's either-or. We either live as if everything is a miracle or as if nothing is.

Since we're just playing here, how are you feeling now? Are you warm? Cold? Is your breathing relaxed? Are you comfortable at the thought of life without miracles?

Would you be willing to live for a week holding onto the belief that life is not a miracle, just to see what that might feel like? It doesn't matter what happens during that week. Pleasant or unpleasant things can happen. You may get the best news you've been waiting for or the worst news that you've been dreading. Whatever happens during the week…just happens.

Now, let's flip the table. Let's assume that *all* of life is a miracle. Does this change your definition of miracle? Does a miracle have to be something out of the ordinary? Does it require setting aside the laws of nature? Can a miracle be something that is laced with wonder, large or small?

Maybe believing that everything is a miracle means living with a mindfulness of the details of life, noticing the synchronicities of life, paying attention to the coincidences, the unexpected, the moments of energy bursts.

If you choose to live life as if everything is a miracle, then you may be overwhelmed with the wonder of if all. For example, in some strange way my fingers know which keys on my keyboard to press (much of the time) to get what thought I'm having down on paper.

How did the thought come into my brain? How do my fingers know how to do that? What is it about this machine I'm using that allows me to create? It's just a box, more or less. There are people who are proficient in their understanding of these boxes, but nevertheless, there is a point beyond which they cannot explain.

When you choose to live as if all of life is a miracle, then you align in mysterious ways with the mysterious—call that God, the universe, chi. You admit that you do not really know much about life and that even when you are not happy with life at the moment, you are willing to hold on until you see the sun peek out from behind the clouds. By the way, how does *that* happen?

When all life is a miracle, things happen that you do not like and...and...then they change. You live with hope because miracles surround you. They are above you, below you, beside you, inside you. They make life an adventure, no matter what is happening. Even pain is a miracle because the pain leads to growth in small or large, ordinary or strange ways.

Stop for a second right now. Do you feel hot? Cold? How's your breathing? Are you tense or relaxed? Try living for a week consciously thinking that everything is a miracle. What happens?

When you get to a certain point on your life journey, this question of everything in life being a miracle or nothing being a miracle becomes more important. Your decision affects your attitude, your sense of value, your openness to face whatever is on your path. You can choose—yes, you really can—how you will proceed through the next hours, days, weeks, months, and years. You may revisit your decision at any time.

Current evidence may point you to the position that nothing in life is a miracle. That's a way to choose to live. Later something may happen that knocks you off your well-planted feet and you decide that everything is a miracle. Or you may decide that all life is a miracle and then you begin to suspect, because of what's going on in your world, that you may be wrong. You reverse your choice.

Keep asking the question of whether everything is a miracle or nothing, no matter which end of the spectrum you choose. Think about it when you're brushing your teeth, driving to the store, preparing a meal, returning messages, getting dressed, waiting in line, or just waking up.

As you live with this challenge from Albert Einstein, watch what happens. If you like what you experience, YAY! If you don't, then let it go. The choice is yours.

With Love,
Your Secret Admirer

4

"Letting go is a process that is seldom easy. For many, its meaning is elusive. How do we 'let go'? Letting go means removing our attention from a particular experience or person and putting our focus on the here and now. We hang on to the past, to past hurts, but also to past jobs. We have to let the past pass. The struggle to hang on to it, any part of it clouds the present. You can't see the possibilities today is offering if your mind is still drawn to what was."

— *Each Day a New Beginning* —

Dear One,

The Hebrew scriptures tell that, once upon a time, there were two wicked cities—Sodom and Gomorrah. They were so bad that God decided they could not be changed for the good and would have to be destroyed. We don't know all the things the residents of those cities did that were so bad. For all we know, the cities may have been the kinds of places you or your friends would like to live in today. But, no matter. Sodom and Gomorrah were going to be destroyed—maybe by a volcano or an earthquake or a raging fire. However, there was one family—Lot's family—that God thought was worth saving.

Two angels visited this family, but Lot didn't realize they were angels. He simply was being hospitable when he invited the two to stay with his family for the evening. This is the way good people did things in those days when there were no motels along the highway.

The angels said they appreciated the invitation but would sleep outside in the city center. But Lot wouldn't hear of that, so the angels spent the night at his house. When morning came, the angels got up and even before breakfast told Lot that he, his wife, and his two daughters needed to leave the city immediately because a great punishment was coming.

The family just stared at the angels and began their usual morning tasks, sweeping the house and preparing meals. But the angels would have none of that lollygagging. They literally grabbed Lot and his family and pushed them out the door. They took the family to the edge of the city and told them to skedaddle. The angels told Lot to run to the hills and not look back. If they did that, they, too, would be destroyed.

Lot still didn't know the two people were angels and he must have been in a daze because instead of hightailing it out of there, he tried to negotiate with the angels.

"I don't want to run to the hills because we might die there," he said. "I'd rather take my family to that city over yonder." He pointed to a spot in the distance. "See that little city? My family will be safe there."

The angels were exasperated by that time, so they agreed that the family could go to the small city and be safe. But they gave a final warning to Lot and his family not to look back. Sodom and Gomorrah were going to be rained on by fire and brimstone, they said. Satisfied with the deal he was finally able to broker, Lot, his wife, and their two daughters, headed toward the little city.

But Lot's wife could not resist the temptation to turn around and look at all they were leaving. She looked at her old life, her old way of being, her old form of security, her old friends, and her old home. She could not let go and, just as the angels had said would happen, she turned into a pillar of salt.

If you don't finally let go of the idea that you can control what's changing around you, you could turn into a pillar of salt, too. You can't always keep your family healthy. Cancer and accidents happen. Eating properly, taking your vitamins, and exercising are no guarantee that you will live to be 100. You cannot control what happens at that committee meeting or what your spouse does or how your parents or your children or grandchildren live their lives. You cannot control what happens at church, in your community, or in your world. You ARE NOT GOD!

You may have to let go of some of your dearly-held beliefs, too. Is the faith that you professed as a child still the faith you affirm today? Do you hear the voices of your parents in your head? Are they still relevant or have you outgrown them? Are you placing too much importance on things that are no longer needful in your life?

As a kid, maybe you finally let go of that security blanket you were so attached to. As a teenager, you let go of the hope that a certain someone would notice you, ask you out, and the two of you would live happily ever after. At a certain point in your life, you let go of the dream to write the great American novel, to be a star on Broadway, to be the perfect spouse, child, sibling, or grandparent. You let go of expectations that life would always be sunny and trouble-free. At least, I hope you did.

Celebrities are prime examples of this refusal to let go. Because they've had so much plastic surgery done, you don't even recognize some who were famous for decades. You understand why they did it, though. Don't you wish some of the photos taken of you had been Photo-shopped before they were posted on Facebook?

A fellow named Paul wrote in a letter to friends in the ancient city of Ephesus: "You were taught to put away your former way of life, your old self, corrupt and deluded by its lusts, and to be renewed in the spirit of your minds, and to clothe yourselves with the new self, created according to the likeness of God..." (Ephesians 4:22-24).

How new might you become when you let go of your attachment to what other people think? What would your world be like if you could let go of rigid interpretations of religion and personal spirituality? How wonderful would it be to let go of your negative emotions—some of those feelings you've been lugging around for years? How different would your personal and communal world be if you didn't feel the need to judge others?

I hope you will let go. I hope you will become a new creation, especially in this time of life. I hope that you will not become a pillar of salt.

With Love,
Your Secret Admirer

5

"Finding meaning does not require us to live differently;
it requires us to see our lives differently."
— *Rachel Naomi Remen* —

Dear One,

You may think that life as you knew it is over.

It is. Something has changed. You are in transition.

If you are getting older, chances are that you no longer have the physical coordination that you had as a young person. Your face shows the evidence of living. Friends have passed.

You don't have zest for certain things as you once did. You no longer feel the need to clean the bathrooms every week or dust more than once a month. You've changed your diet, eliminating gluten and dairy. You feel like a background player in the drama of other people's lives and only rarely do you get a speaking part.

Your eyes don't function as well as they once did. You ask people on occasion to repeat what they said. You prefer comfortable shoes rather than stylish, stiff, tight ones.

You don't know many of the people nominated at the awards shows for television, movies, and music. Even when you think you recognize them, you can't remember their names.

You no longer report to work every morning, every week, every month of the year. You do not drive much after dark. You decided that getting a good night sleep was more important than sharing a bedroom with a spouse who snores. You now have your own room just as your lover has personal space.

So yes, in some ways, life as you knew it *is* over. But the changes aren't all bad. Now you can decide how your life will be full in a different way. When you let some things go, when you experience loss, you will find that you have new choices. You can decide how you want to think about these things. You can decide what new vision your life presents you.

You may no longer have the physical coordination that you once had, but you can walk with more intention. You can see the caterpillar on the tree limb over the sidewalk. You can think about how your body moves as you get into a car. You can decide to sign up for a Tai Chi class with a friend—improving your balance while at the same of time deepening a relationship with someone.

You may meet new people who soon become friends. You can slow down rather than running everywhere, not seeing or paying attention. You can actually enjoy the world around you, because you will notice things…maybe for the first time in a long time.

Yes, the face you see in the mirror has more wrinkles than the face of the 30-year-old woman who used to look at you. Believe it or not, you can be grateful for those wrinkles. You can see your grandmother's eyes now when you look into the mirror. You can see your father and *his* father when you look at your neck. You can see other relatives come through as your body continues to change.

And when you look at the generations who follow you, you can see your family in their faces, expressions, and movements as well. With each wrinkle, you can appreciate the continuity that becomes evident. Only you will know the wonder of this gift.

You have lost dear friends…to Alzheimer's, a brain tumor, a heart attack, cancer. Some of your childhood friends have already died and you miss them. You wish you had been with them more during their last days instead of being "too busy" to be there.

Maybe you were afraid of getting too close because it felt like dying was catching, that if you focused on it too much it might come to visit you as well. Then again, maybe it just hurt too much to watch someone you loved go away. You can choose to be alone or, though it takes time and is risky, you can decide to reach out and make new friends.

Yes, it takes effort to make contact and then to nurture those connections. These new friends, too, may die before you. The friends you now grieve walked with you through personal challenges. Those trials have passed along with your friends.

Your new friends will not be weighed down with some of the heavy issues of before. You can build with them new memories, be there for each other in new ways, share new ideas, new challenges, and new joys. You can help each other explore each other's uncharted journeys. You can laugh, cry, and scream together.

You can choose to live your life differently, yet build on the strengths, support, and laughter of your former friends. Your deceased friends taught you the value of deep friendship. You can search that out again.

Perhaps you don't clean your home as frequently as you did. Good for you! There are not as many people living in your house now so there are probably not as many messes. You have realized that your time can be spent in ways beyond mandating a dust cloth over the furniture every week, but you've also learned that inviting people over can be a wonderful motivation for cleaning your house. When you are in the mood to clean, you can fully engage in the process and enjoy it.

You've changed your diet, based on your doctor's recommendation. Perhaps you can't graze as freely at the buffet table at wedding receptions, but you can delight in finding restaurants with gluten-free menus.

Given your new food restrictions, people think about you more as they plan their menus for book club, meetings, and family gatherings. There's something special about that. Admit it. Changing your eating habits has improved your health and your general outlook on life. Yes, it took some work, but it's much better than taking a handful of pills! And, whether you see it or not, you look healthier, too. You've lost weight and you have more energy for living. What a different way to perceive your "deprivation"!

Your children are now grown and able to handle their own lives. Did you imagine that they would continue to depend on you? Well, maybe you hoped they might, but you raised them to be independent and they are, which is to your credit.

They have spouses and children and work and home and community activities and friends. They live across town or hours away. As a parent, you'd like to believe that you are still central in their lives. You're not, and it hurts. However, because your children no longer need your undivided attention, you have time and space in your life for things you couldn't do before. You can more completely embrace your spouse, your friends, previously declined social engagements, new adventures, even time alone.

You know that if your children really needed you, they'd call. Obviously, they are running their lives as well as you did at their ages. Keep in touch as you need to, and rejoice that your children are launched into their own lives with their own challenges and ways of doing things.

You no longer hurry to the store for the most current fashions, especially since most are designed for people younger than you. You can still wear clothes that are stylish and comfortable without dressing like your younger neighbor or your older parent.

Finally, you can find your own style. People are not going to look at how you are dressed like they once did. In some ways, you are now invisible to younger people. That can be wonderful. Remember the poem about getting old and wearing purple and a red hat? Celebrate that freedom!

You're thinking more about retirement…or starting to and it scares you. Change your vocabulary. Rather than thinking of yourself as retiring, consider the possibility that you're redesigning! You can do nothing…or everything you've dreamed of. You can try things you didn't have time for before…beginning a new business, volunteering, traveling, spending time with friends or family members, sleeping in late, meditating, exercising, fishing, learning to play an instrument, coloring, doing jigsaw puzzles, lying around reading all day. You have the gift of deciding how you'll spend your days. You will decide that—not a boss!

Life will continue to change. It's up to you. You can bemoan what is no more or you can decide to look at your life now and redefine your new normal. Change the lenses in your glasses from this-is-the-way-things-were to this-is-the-way-things-are and life is good.

With love,
Your Secret Admirer

6

"Sometimes we must leave our fixed abode and become sojourners in uncertainty. We need to learn that no place, however hallowed in our memories, is more holy than any other."

— *Elizabeth Watson* —

Dear One,

At one time or another, you will leave who you have been. You may leave a home of many years. You may be considering a new job. You may even be contemplating how to clear out clutter to make space for whatever is next to come.

When I speak of these things, I am not speaking just of "things." Even so, have you noticed that when you clean out your closet, you almost immediately find new clothes you like better, that are more stylish, and that fit you better? Maybe you found clothes hidden in the closet that you had forgotten and were able to put together totally new outfits using items that were already there. You had not realized that that shirt looked so good with those pants and that jacket and you're delighted!

That's the way life is. We let go of some things to make room for something else that is equally special.

Sometimes what you decide to let go of are painful memories. You may continue to hear a person's voice in your head, undermining your self-confidence. You may be afraid to tackle something new because of fears instilled long ago. Maybe you've wanted to learn something new and you never signed up for the class because you still hear that teacher criticize your efforts many years in the past.

Is that teacher still in the room? Does that teacher even live on your street? In the same town? If not, then whose voice are you actually hearing?

That's right. It's not the teacher's. It's your own voice now. Since the voice is yours, you can decide right now to change the tape. You can accept with compassion that you once had this thought and you can return it to where it belongs—in the past, which does not exist anymore.

As Queen Elizabeth I once said, the past cannot be cured. It's gone. Over. You can acknowledge the past and its effects on you up till now…and then open your hand and blow it away like the seeds of a dandelion. You can remember feeling the pain or fear. You can even be grateful and bless the pain or fear because it may have helped you at the time. But you no longer have to allow those negative energies to affect who you are now. You have left that abode and are now in a different place.

In your early adult years, you probably moved several times. You were able to create a home in each apartment or house, no matter how tiny or temporary. You may still have photos lying around where your family or friends were at one of those dwellings. But those places are no longer part of your reality. Where you are—your current home—is your reality.

Perhaps you miss things about other places you've lived—the location of one, the funky bathtub of another, the walk-in closet of another? But now, you can't imagine living any place else.

And yet, you know, too, that sometime soon you may need to move closer to your children or to a facility that can provide some assistance you need. You will hold onto fond memories of where you live now, but, as before, you will make your new dwelling place home.

If you find it necessary to move elsewhere, it may be difficult for a time. You will have to decide what items to keep, what to give to family, what to give to thrift stores, what to throw away. It will take you a while to learn new routines, to have other people in your life (sometimes demanding to make your decisions for you), and to learn where things are.

But a new life is there waiting for you. You'll meet new people and have more chances to do fun things without having to plan the event, drive there, and clean up afterwards.

Sometimes the fixed abode that you are called to leave is not a place but a way of thinking about yourself and the support system around you. If you worked your entire life, when you retire, you lose some of your friends and your social network. Sure, you all can decide to get together monthly or quarterly but that is different from seeing each other in the hall or grabbing a quick cup of coffee together.

You may feel lost for a while. But you will find people to go to movies with, eat with, talk over family issues with, or try new things with.

You used to say, "Hi, I'm [your name] and I'm a medical technician at [name of the facility.]" Now that no longer applies.

How will you now introduce yourself? As a *former* medical technician? As a community volunteer? As a caregiver? As an explorer in this adventure of life? How will you describe yourself to others?

The most important parts of your identity will change over time. Perhaps after being a parent for 25 years, you've seen your children go to college or marry and get on with their lives. Currently you may be an active grandparent to young grandchildren. Later you may be a visitor to shut-ins at your church. Each step along this uncharted journey may require a new assessment of what to tell others when you put out your hand and say, "Hello."

You will experience grief over losing your former way of life. You may begin to feel as if you will always be alone or friendless. That's okay. All people do. Let yourself experience those feelings. And be open to new people entering your life. But remember that they won't if you sit at home and wait for someone to come knocking on your door!

In your solitude, you can open your heart to God's guidance. You can tell Steadfast Love that you'd like new people in your life. You can begin conversations with the cashier at the grocery store. If you attend church, you can intentionally sit on a different pew and talk with different people. You can call people you have found interesting and ask if they'd like to meet you for coffee so you can get to know them better. The worst thing they can say is no.

You may find yourself spending more time with just yourself. Thomas Merton, a Trappist monk, spent twenty-seven years learning the challenges and joys of solitude. His writings speak of the profound joy of discovering the Holy One in the smallest details of life—details that often get squeezed out when we surround ourselves with noise and people.

Do not be too quick to divert your attention away from learning who you are at this stage of life. You can spend your time frantically trying to fill every moment…just like you did when you were in the workforce, raising a family, active in the community, and socializing with your spouse. This time of life gives you permission to let go of filling your time with *doing* and begin to fill your time with *being*.

Just *being* may be forced upon you by significant changes in your health. Your good health, a dependable body, and a cogent mind begin slipping away. It can be a horrifying thought that you can no longer do what you used to do. You may be embarrassed by what is happening to you, especially when you cannot immediately recall the name of someone you know well. You feel as if you are living in a distant country where you don't know the language. People are speaking in a foreign tongue, forcing you to learn new vocabulary: radiation, biogenics, psychotropic, rollater, etc. It's a scary time.

And yet, there is the possibility that as you adapt to the reality that this is your new normal, you will find joy and peace even amid pain and anxiety about the unknown. You may delight in the fact that someone bathes you, that it feels good to be coddled as when you were a newborn. You may discover that this new life is holy. Yes, holy in a different way from when you were younger but holy, sacred. You have time to meditate on what God has now placed in your lap. You can learn the freedom of allowing others to care for you when you need it, rather than always being the caregiver or person in charge.

You can know that you are not God; you are not in charge of the world, or even of how your life is unfolding. That's not always such a bad thing…as long as you are willing to search for the pearl in the oyster.

Oysters are really ugly. Can you imagine what the early human thought when he or she ate that first raw oyster? It was slimy and looked like the stuff that came out of the nose. Harvesting oysters, after the first people learned the oysters were adequate food, was tricky. The shells could easily slice open a leg. A person could die from the infection.

And yet, people persisted. If birds could eat oysters, so could the ancestors. Then every once in a while, the early human found a white ball in the oyster. It may have just been garbage and so was thrown back into the sea. But along the way, pearls became valuable to humans. Jesus even told a story about a man who sold everything he had to purchase a pearl of great price.

This may be what life is like. You spend a lot of time harvesting oysters. You developed a taste for the meat. This was your life. Until one day, you discovered that something very special had come out of your former life.

You discovered pearls. The next stages of life may be lustrous pearls, more beautiful than the blob of oyster meat that has satisfied you to this point. This next stage is holy, special, never to come again.

Cherish it.

With love,
Your Secret Admirer

7

"I am sixty-four years old. I have fathered children. I have written books. I have letters after my name and an ecclesiastical title before it. I can get into movies and motels at a reduced rate. But to call me an adult or grown-up is an oversimplification at best and a downright misnomer at worst. I am not a past participle but a present participle, even a dangling participle. I am not a having-grown-up one but a growing-up one, a groping-up one, not even sure much of the time just where my growing and groping are taking me or where they are supposed to be taking me. I am a verbal adjective in search of a noun to latch onto, a grower in search of a self to grow into. As far as the outer world is concerned, my acne cleared up around 1945, but in terms of my inner world, it is still with me to add to my general embarrassment and confusion about myself."

— *Frederick Buechner* —

Dear One,

Do you still wonder who you'll be when you grow up?

You realize that you have less time than you used to. And yet, you still wish you could try out some jobs that you didn't do when you were younger. When you were younger, you were too busy trying to create a career for yourself to take a job that paid paltry wages.

Maybe you wished you could be an actress or wanted to try out a medical career. You imagined yourself being the loving grandparent that you used to read about in the novels you devoured as a kid. You wanted to become an adventurer. You wanted to learn graphic design and great knowledge of all things technological. When will you get around to becoming this person?

Some people act as if you've already crossed over that peak of life and that you're sliding down...quickly. Maybe you are. Do you feel as if you are already a "has-been"? Well, in some ways you are. You are a has-been parent to young children. You are a has-been young executive. You are a has-been young spouse.

Maybe you want to enjoy the slide like the one in the playground down the street. And maybe you're not ready for that downward slide. The reality is...you're still growing. You're still learning. You now have time to wonder about why some birds walk on the ground and some hop. You have time to meditate on inspirational readings, to read the same passage over and over until it releases today's truth for you.

You can decide what kind of grandparent you want to be. Will you be one who is always there, talking with children and grandchildren every day, attending sporting events and recitals and plays? Or will you be a grandparent who enjoys your children when they choose to be with you, who allows plenty of space in the relationship when that's what the children want or need? Can you allow yourself to be one way for now and another way next month or year?

Will you ask for what you want and then be content to allow the other person to adhere to your wish or ignore it, while still maintaining a loving relationship? Will you read books you've never read just because you're interested in the topic or because you enjoy "zoning out" with certain types of literature? Will you decide that you're never going to read all those books on your shelves and begin getting rid of them?

Do you choose to live your life as a has-been? Would you rather continue to grow, change, and redefine yourself? What will you do when other people decide you're a has-been? Will you accept their opinion of you as truth? Will you get angry and push them out of your life? Will you decide if there are things you are willing to accept from them and others that you refuse...adamantly?

You may carry around some of the little child dreams inside of you. For reasons that made sense at the time, you decided to put aside those dreams. Now you can open that box, bring them into the light, breathe new breath into them, and watch them grow. For example, maybe when you were a child, you'd hide in your closet and hope that someone in your family would miss you and seek to find you. You no longer have to hide. You can claim what you want, knowing that the other person may not respond the way you choose. Now, though, you know that the response or non-response of the other will not destroy you. You have lived long enough to know that if that person won't seek you, someone else will.

When you allow yourself to acknowledge that you want someone to care enough about you to look for you to be in their lives and then wait calmly and patiently, a person will show up. You may get a phone call or run into someone on your way out of a restaurant. A conversation may begin at church.

You may need to initiate the building of the relationship at first, but you know that you are fulfilling your dream to have someone care about you enough to seek you out. Whoever is seeking you needs you in his/her life as much as you need him/her. The needs may be for different reasons, but you can count on the knowledge that the seeking is a two-way process, with one of you taking the lead for a time and then the other assuming that role.

You may want to create a kind of business card for yourself to hand to people so they will later remember your name, phone number, and e-mail address along with other social media contact addresses you have. You may have noticed that your memory is not what it used to be. Chances are that other people's memory may need some prompts, too.

Do you think about what gives you pleasure, makes you feel special, satisfies your need to feel alive? When you do claim these ideas of pleasure, specialness, and aliveness, cherish them. Give them room to poke their heads into your life and then pull them close to you.

You are at a point in life where you can allow yourself to become who you've known all along you are. You may have kept this awareness of yourself in a chest with the lid locked and pushed deep into a closet because you knew that other people—parents, friends, teachers, pastors, or doctors—would not encourage you. Now you can listen to your own voice and the voice of your inner wisdom. You can take tiny steps toward being the person you have always known you are.

You have as much growth potential in yourself as you did when you were three, thirty-three or older. You are not a has-been in what really matters…the person you were created to be.

Relish this time of your life. Listen to your own truth. Grow with love and joy and delight and purpose, no matter what is happening the world around you. This is your time to BE!

With Love,
Your Secret Admirer

8

"We cannot help the birds of sadness flying over our heads,
but we need not let them build nests in our hair."
— *Chinese saying* —

Dear One,

Years ago, when girls teased their hair and used cases of
hair spray to keep their hair styles a mile high, a story went
around about a girl who finally got her hairdo the way she
wanted it. Every night she wrapped it in toilet paper so that
she wouldn't ruin it in while she slept. In the morning, she
touched it up a bit by sticking the pointed end of a comb into
her hair and then added more hairspray.

One day as she sat in her desk at school, a roach crawled
out of her hair. And then another one appeared. Of course, she
screamed and ran, in tears, from the room. The boys laughed,
and the girls scratched their heads and ran their fingers
through the stiff mountains on their heads to make sure the
same infestation had not occurred in their crowning glories.

Some days are filled with dread, doubt, despair, and
despondency. Maybe you don't feel good physically. Maybe you
have a cold or your knee hurts or you're worried that the spot
on your face may be cancer.

Some days you wake up and remember those folks who died unexpectedly—your friend's mother-in-law who dropped dead the day following her birthday when she was happy and in good health; your co-worker's father who died after being ill only twelve hours; your dog that got run over by a car.

You fear that you will find your spouse dead in his bed one morning or you'll get a call that your mother found your dad dead out in the garden. You fear that death can come to you or someone you love unexpectedly and without warning. You just don't think you can face a day when such things might happen.

Some days you doubt that anyone really cares about you. You haven't heard from your family or your friends in a while—a few days, a few weeks, a few months. You wonder if anyone cares whether you are alive. You even called an adult child just to say that you're alive and the humor was lost on the fruit of your loins! You doubt that if you needed help there would be someone to step forward.

Some days you are filled with despair. The world as you knew it is no more. The actions of the government dismay you. Your favorite grocery store no longer carries the brand of mayonnaise that you have eaten for years. Your body betrays you. You wonder if that twinge in your chest is just gas or the beginnings of a heart attack. The ache in your hand could be crippling arthritis or simply overwork from working in the yard yesterday. The support circle upon whom you relied has moved, is involved with grandchildren and/or aging parents, or has health issues.

What is this world coming to? With the body you have, you may never want to put on a swimsuit again. Your hair won't go into the style you have worn for the last forty years. The faith of your youth no longer seems to sustain you as it once did. Why are people so caught up into acts of hatred? (Maybe you need to turn off the television for a while. Do not even watch Law and Order while you are in this dark place of despair.)

Your spouse seems to take you for granted. No longer do you receive flowers for no reason. The climate is changing in ways that are not good for the planet or for human beings.

Yes, some days are just like that. Everywhere you turn, you experience darkness of spirit.

Dear One, that's okay. Of course, you will occasionally feel dread, doubt, despair, and despondency. You will feel these emotions because of things that actually happen in your life and because of things you imagine may happen. Whether they're real or not, your *feelings* are real. You are the guest of honor at your own pity party. When you choose to throw yourself such an event, I want you to make it a magnificent occurrence.

Make sure that you do not invite any other guests so that you can enjoy your distress all alone for this one day. Plan for plenty of tears. The dress code is informal—even pajamas all day if that makes the party work for you. And your hair? Forget about it. You did not invite a photographer to this pity party so what difference does it make if your hair is flat against your head in places and stands up in others?

Let's see, for refreshments, you can either put yourself on bread and water all day (gluten-free bread if you need that) or you can go to the other extreme and eat all those calorie rich, off-the-diet foods you keep on hand. Please, no beer, wine, or liquor. That's not a good beverage for a pity party. How about cups of nice, hot tea? Maybe some of those herbal ones so you will not get jacked up on caffeine.

One more thing. No computer, telephone, or tablet. No zoning out with Facebook, You Tube, or gaming. This is a party for you to wallow around with your dread, doubt, despair, and despondency. If necessary, you can color invitations or decorations for your party. You may want to write in your journal or make collages as part of the entertainment. You want your pity party to get a five-star rating as far as parties go.

Then…after the party…you can decide how you want to handle your dread. Yes, people die unexpectedly. Just because someone's mother-in-law died unexpectedly does not mean that someone close to you will. And yet, it can happen. You may indeed get that phone call that you dread so much. If you do, then what? Allow your dread today to be an impetus to think through how you would handle such an event.

For example, if, as you sometimes dread, you find your spouse dead, what will you do? Figure out now who you will call. Make sure you have those phone numbers in a place you can easily access. Is there any information that you need to gather? Things such as which mortuary to call or financial or legal professionals to contact? Do you know which family members or friends you would call to be with you? What if they do not answer their phones? After your plans are made, put them in writing and place the document on a shelf or in a drawer where you can find them and then forget them. You've addressed your immediate fears. Now, relax.

If all this seems gruesome, then don't do it, but when you find yourself watching the television show in your brain where you find your spouse on the floor dead, turn off the television. Stop your thoughts of worrying about finding your loved one dead or almost dead. By living in the middle of this horrific dread, you are cutting yourself off from your loved one. It's hard to stay connected to the one you love when you fear that the one you love may do something like this...to you!

When you doubt that anyone cares about you...child, friend, neighbor, or spouse, this is the time...after the pity party...to call or invite someone to go for a walk with you or suggest that two of you go out to eat. If no one is available (maybe it's a holiday or the person is filled with other responsibilities that have nothing to do with you), then take yourself on a date.

Take yourself to a movie or to a restaurant. Initiate a conversation with the wait staff. Go to a shop and talk with a clerk. Maybe the clerk is having a lousy day and your kind words and personal interest may be just the antidote needed.

You can always write a note (yes, people still do that with real paper and a stamp!). Write someone you love and tell them. Or think of someone who probably feels alone and isolated (do you recognize that feeling?), write a note of compassion, and put it in the mail. Imagine the look of amazement on the face of the recipient of your act of kindness.

After the pity party, if despair is what you still feel, you may choose to put yourself on a news diet. You do not have to keep up with all the news of the day or the week. Stop allowing the trauma of the world to enter your personal world for a time.

So, what if you don't know what the latest action the president took or what the hot Hollywood starlet did! The world can survive without your knowing about the events going on around the globe.

Does this seem harsh? News "junkies" might find it disastrous to put themselves on such a diet. But there are people who do not watch the news feeds on all the media devices and who do not read the newspaper...and they survive. You might try it. Rather than filling your mind and your spirit with all the negative things going on in the world, look for the good things instead.

If what you are despairing about is your health, go to the doctor. Don't let your imagination run wild. Get that skin spot checked out. Put heat and ice on your knee and if it is still sore after a few days, go to a medical practitioner.

Some people find it comforting to add alternative health practices to their regular traditional medical regimen. You may decide that getting massages regularly soothes your body and spirit. There are other options: reiki, acupuncture, craniosacral therapy, aroma therapy and a host of others. Especially if you live alone, having someone else help your body function at its maximum is nurturing in itself.

I hope I don't need to remind you that good nutrition, exercise, and not smoking also help alleviate some of your dread. But... and this is a BIG but...even when you take care of yourself, you may indeed experience a health issue that you would rather avoid. If that is the case, then learn to live, truly live, *with* it—don't let it determine what your mood will be. I'll write more about this in another letter.

Sadness, despair, dread, distress, and despondency will fly over your head. You can choose how to deal with them. But, don't let roaches grow in your hair. Clean out the debris and decide to keep your head, heart, mind, and spirit open to other ways of choosing to live your life.

With love,
Your Secret Admirer

9

"When I am constantly running, there is no time for being. When there is no time for being there is no time for listening."
— *Madeleine L'Engle* —

Dear One,

You have been so busy with life. You can be proud of all that you have accomplished in the community and with your friends and family. Your To-Do lists are wonderful to behold. They have a nice balance of things that are important and urgent. You include "clean out the refrigerator," "make reservations for the weekend trip," "write letter to the editor," and "spend time with family" all on the same list. You see your lists as a glorious game plan. Your lists help you to remember the things you want to do, the things you do not want to forget. They help you maintain the details of life. Good for you. You are reliable, you do what you tell someone you will do. You are trustworthy.

Your calendar stays full—maybe not as full as it once did—and you keep the white spaces filled with all kinds of activities, responsibilities, and entertainments. You feel important when people want to spend time with you over coffee or when your presence or expertise is important to a group of people in a meeting. You are thrilled when a family member or friend asks you to be present at a special event for them. When these kinds of things happen, you know you're not invisible, that your life has meaning for other people, that you matter.

You plan for exercise, reading holy writings, and meditating on spiritual readings. You structure your day for good hygiene, nutritious eating, and sleep. You even keep a record of how many hours of sleep that you get each night.

If you have nothing on your To-Do list that is immediately pressing, you may spend time, maybe hours, on your computer, using social media or playing games. Is this called "zoning out?"

You are busy even though you do not define yourself that way. You know that being busy is not necessarily the best way to prove your worth to yourself or someone else. When an acquaintance asks, "Are you keeping busy these days?" you know that simply saying "yes" is really not an answer at all. So you reply, "I'm keeping busy enough."

Do you fear that if you answered, "No, I'm not busy," people would devalue you, think you were boring, or feel pity for you?

You spend your time doing. You have lots of activities and interests. Are you afraid that if you stop, you will vegetate into a turnip? You will be unworthy to live, to walk this earth?

Do you think that if you take time for yourself to do nothing, you will be selfish? That others will cluck their tongues and wonder what is wrong with you? That you will be cast aside because you are not "pulling your weight," you're no longer the good ole dependable you?

If any of those things are true, you probably stay busy. You keep doing. You do kind things for others, you help with others' projects, you always say yes when a family member or friend asks for some of your time. You run from this appointment to another, from this responsibility to another, from this entertainment to another, from this cause to another, from this church meeting or volunteer opportunity to another, from this computer game to another. You run and run so you will not be caught.

Running around when you were a kid felt good. Maybe you still literally run as an adult. Running can be good for your health. When you were a child, running meant being outside, away from the confines of parental supervision. Running meant escaping from your friends who wanted to tickle you until you wet your pants. Running meant you breathed hard and filled your lungs. That activity felt deeply good and exhilarating. Physical running can give you time to meditate, to unwind, to let go of the stresses in life.

Staying busy, figuratively running without stopping, can be bad for your health: physically, emotionally, and spiritually. You run and run so that whatever is trying to be born in you now cannot catch you. You will not stop because... because you may acknowledge a loss, realize there are parts of your life you want to/need to let go, and you may begin to grow in new ways.

This new growth cannot happen when you are busy, busy, busy. You do not have time for it. You can't afford it. You are afraid of it. New growth may have risks. New growth usually requires letting go of something that has been important to this point but is no longer nurturing. New growth comes from loss, loss of things that used to matter to you but are no longer essential to your well-being.

The problem is that the running track is hard to get off. You cannot find the exit gate. You keep hearing the crowds cheer even though you are covered in dirt, your clothes are soaked in sweat, you are gasping for breath, your feet hurt, you are super thirsty, and your eyes are so blurry that you cannot see the finish line, or even if there is a finish line. So you run and run and run.

You may want to reduce the busyness but the pressures of friends, family, business colleagues, church members, and your own image of yourself forbid you to stop.

I'm telling you now: STOP. The universe, God, Life, has a way of stopping you so you can do what is essential for your essence, your soul, your spirit. If you cannot stop your busyness on your own, and I'll admit that can be hard to do, you will be stopped...for your own good. You may get sick, you may experience a kind of darkness in your spirit, you may lose your job or your financial security. I'm not telling you this as a threat. I'm telling you because I yearn for you to find your ultimate meaning for your life and you WILL NOT find it by staying busy and by filling your time frantically doing good, taking care of others, or even being wicked. You need time to just...be.

When you stop, whether by your choice or because it is forced upon you, use this time to rest in God, in Steadfast Love, in the Goodness of Grace. Allow yourself to "float," to reflect upon how the world is still functioning even without you racing around in it. Listen to music that speaks to your innermost being. For a time, even avoid your hobbies, especially if they allow you to produce (a completed jigsaw puzzle, a collage or painting, a pristine garden, a book read to the end.) Eventually, soon, these will be helpful to you but at first, just rest in the arms of a loving God. Allow yourself to be enough. You are enough for now, sitting in the sun, enjoying the birds pecking in the dirt. You are enough for now, breathing in life's goodness. You are enough for now sitting beside a loved one, without talking. You are enough eating nutritious, delicious food, really savoring it, enjoying the tastes and textures. You are enough. Just be a being. Remember during this initial time of weaning yourself from always running, busily, that you are a human *being*, not a human *doer*!

When you stop, then slowly, slowly, maybe in a week, maybe in a month, maybe in a year, you will be able to listen, to hear what is next for you. You will be able to see what joyous thing is coming next. It may be tiny, as when you finally perfect that biscuit recipe that you've never taken the time to try and try again. You may hear an off-hand comment that someone makes that lights up your imagination and opens a new world of opportunity for you. You may discover a deep well of wisdom that people begin to seek out in you. An important relationship may find new depths of love and caring. Who knows what you'll explore when you eliminate the noise of your previous life and sit in the now of this time, listening, paying attention, and being open to whatever is now coming to you?

The past is gone. The future is the future. Now is when you can listen, when you stop your running.

With Love,
Your Secret Admirer

10

"Life is a long preparation for something that never happens."
— *William Butler Yeats* —

Dear One,

Have you ever feared something...like getting bitten by a dog, running out of money, or urinating in your pants in public? How did those fears affect how you lived?

Because of your fear, do you hold off doing something fun or crazy until you win the lottery even though you currently have more resources than you need to meet your everyday expenses? Maybe there is a trip you want to take, a college scholarship you want to fund, or a painter you want to support by purchasing a piece of her art, but you don't do any of these things because you're afraid that you'll run out of money before you run out of days.

Have you avoided public gatherings because you're afraid you'll wet your pants? Have you missed speakers you yearned to hear, street festivals that celebrated the joy of your community, or hugging a special child because you were afraid you would have "an accident"?

Maybe these things have happened to you...once...maybe twice. But how have these fears plus many others held you back from experiencing the richness of life's fullness? Do you no longer enjoy swimming because of how you think you look in a swimsuit?

When you were young, what career did you prepare for? If you went to college, what did you major in? Is the course of study you labored over all those years ago the actual groundwork of what you did last year or even ten years ago? Did you major in mathematics only to turn out to be a minister? Did you prepare to be a business manager only to discover that you really wanted to be a teacher? Did you plan on going into the family business only to have that business collapse, requiring you to discover another path?

Did you plan the path that led you to where you are today? Did you plan your career path, your community involvement experiences, your significant relationships, who your children or grandchildren are today? Did you?

Did you expend a lot of energy trying to make things happen that never did, never will? Did you do everything in your power to guarantee your grandchild would have a good life only to discover that he got involved with drugs? Or take a child with disabilities to doctor after doctor, clinic after clinic, trying to "fix" the problem and ignored the wonderful person this child is? Perhaps all your efforts denied the reality that your child's spirit was stronger than you could even imagine. Finally, one day you embraced your child as the perfect person she is even though she may never be able to live independently.

Maybe you planned, built, and decorated your dream home only to discover that it did not fulfill your deep yearnings...or maybe it burned down. After the shock of the loss, you realized that you were not really very sad. What you enjoyed was the planning and dreaming, not the actual living in the house.

Maybe you planned your financial future with the expectation that you would continue working the same job until you retired but then the company was sold or your job became obsolete. You floundered with the question of your long-term financial situation.

You plan and plan and plan. Rarely do things turn out as you planned. Ending every plan with "God willing" may be a healthy way to think about life. For example, a friend may ask you to meet him for coffee one morning later in the week and you answer, "I'll be there, God willing." You certainly intend to spend time with your friend but…you get invited to go out of town at the last minute, you get sick, you have an accident, another friend needs you to drive her to the doctor, or you oversleep. You planned for something…that never happened! The grandfather of a friend always said, "God willing and the creek don't rise!" whenever he committed to something or made a plan.

Life is not an If-Then proposition. If I do this, then that will happen. As much as you want to think life works that way, it just does not. If you've been struggling with an illness for a long time, you may not have expected to still be alive. Or you may never have expected to lose your hearing or to need a walker. You planned to be limber forever by exercising and taking vitamins. But life did not turn out as you planned.

Have you planned and planned for something that never happened? *Dear One*, you can waste so many of your precious hours, weeks, months, and days planning and preparing for things that never happen. This can make you feel crazy and maybe it is delusional…trying to be God. You cannot control the future any more than you can change the past.

Getting that concept into your head and heart can be difficult. You want control. You want to be in charge of the world...or if not the world, at least the lives of your loved ones and yourself.

Maybe one way you can release this need to make the future come out the way you have planned it is to say to yourself, "When I am queen/king of the world, then I will..." You know you're *not* the queen of the world, so let go of the "edict" you would make.

A current thing some people say when someone challenges them is, "Whatever." This word usually ends an argument or distasteful conversation. But, what if you decided that when you said, "Whatever" you really meant it? In other words, what if you let "whatever" happen, accept it as life and move on?

If you are a person of faith, *Whatever* is a way of releasing the present to a Being beyond your limited bounds of control. *Whatever* allows you to enjoy the present without fretting over what happened before or what is coming next. You will deal with it no matter what "it" is.

You may not have dealt with issues so well in the past. Even so, you learned some valuable lessons, so you can alter your actions, beliefs, or thoughts today. You are stronger, wiser, and more adept because of your past. So, go ahead and say it.

Whatever.

Allow yourself to quit worrying, excessively preparing, and ignoring what is now in front of you. You will cope or celebrate, depending on what comes next on your uncharted journey.

With love,
Your Secret Admirer

11

"Be gracious to me, O Lord, for I am in distress; my eye wastes away from grief, my soul and body also. For my life is spent with sorrow, and my years with sighing; my strength fails because of my misery, and my bones waste away. I am the scorn of all my adversaries, a horror to my neighbors, an object of dread to my acquaintances; those who see me in the street flee from me. I have passed out of mind like one who is dead; I have become like a broken vessel. For I hear the whispering of many—terror all around!—as they scheme together against me, as they plot to take my life."

— Psalm 31: 9-13 —

Dear One,

Sometimes you just need a good, big, sloppy feel-sorry-for-yourself party. If you need some help getting started, look at the words the psalmist wrote in Psalm 31. Those four verses cover a lot of pain and damage: grief, poor health, loss of friends, invisibility, and fear. I find it amazing that a book that talks about people's relationship and understanding of God has this kind of raw language in it.

I'm going to give the psalmist a name. I'll call him Robert. Robert has lost someone or some dream that was dearly held. He has wept so much with grief that his eyes can't even focus. He is blinded by his tears. His misery has drained his energy and his strength. He is stooped over because his bones are no longer strong enough to keep him standing upright. Robert is overwhelmed with his grief and the suffering seems to be very longstanding.

Robert's friends are not comfortable being with him because his grief is too difficult for them to be around. Some of them have told him that his grief has been going on long enough and that he needs to pull himself together. They have given up on him. They have done all they can and will do. His acquaintances feel they need to get on with their lives and so they begin to ignore Robert. It doesn't happen all at once, but Robert begins to notice that fewer and fewer people come to visit or call him. He realizes that they have written him off or forgotten him. So now feelings of abandonment by his friends compound his deep sorrow. He feels as if he may as well be dead. It seems that he is invisible to the world. He even becomes a bit paranoid fearing that his own life is in danger, either from others or his own hand.

You can relate to Robert. Go ahead and wallow in your grief for a time. When you get ready, then cry out as Robert eventually did. He said, "But I trust in you, O LORD; I say, 'You are my God'" (Psalm 31:14). Find that Being, that Reality, that is greater than you are and release your pain there. Trust and hope that life is more than what you are currently experiencing. You are stronger than you believe. Hope, trust, and let go when you are ready. Life is waiting.

With love,
Your Secret Admirer

12

"We cannot live the afternoon of life according to the program of life's morning—for what was great in the morning will be little at evening, and what in the morning was true will at evening have become a lie."

— Carl Jung —

Dear One,

Maybe you're comfortable with the way you look.

Good for you.

However, do you ever look at pictures of yourself when you were young? Do you remember how, when you were your younger self, you wished that you looked differently?

You thought your legs looked skinny or fat. You despaired that your hair would not cooperate to being arranged in the current style. Do you sometimes wish now for those skinny legs or slightly plump legs? Do you mourn the loss of that thick, lush hair? Or do you still wear your hair the way you did in high school or exercise like crazy to get that 16-year-old body back?

How much do you spend on anti-aging products? Do they work? Is there room in your bathroom vanity for any more products that, like so many others, do not fulfill their promises? Do you try to become again the person you once were?

Are you trying to live life as you once did...when you had energy to burn or when your house was always immaculate or when you had a job that paid well or when all your family was still living at home or when Sunday School answers to life's problems made sense?

What are you holding onto from your younger self? Where are you not letting go of old ideas, prejudices, and assumptions? How are the rules and expectations that worked so well for you in the past now failing you? Are you still trying to live in yesterday's morning when you are living in the afternoon today?

It is sometimes hard to acknowledge that the person you were is no longer you. But, *Dear One*, that can be very, very good. Think of the pressures you felt to succeed in school or in your job. Do you still need to feel those pressures now that you are living in a different time of your life? Maybe some of the people you worked so hard to please—parents, teachers, bosses, spouses, children, friends, and even people you hardly knew—are no longer around. You may discover that they are not concerned with whether you are perfect or that you meet their every need. And those who do still expect you to be the person you used to be will just have to learn that *that* person no longer lives in your body—if indeed she ever did!

Maybe when you were younger, you had dreams of being …what? The top of your field? Parent of the year? In the Hall of Fame? Best-selling author? Owner of the yard of the month? Guru to the stars? Do you still strive for those acclamations? Is it time to let some of them go so you can discover what you really want to do, who you really are, and which awards you want to give to yourself? Maybe you will discover that the social creature you once were now yearns to be the contemplative, quiet person who pays attention to the internal world rather than the external one. Or you realize that the things you stressed about don't really matter anymore. So, what if you don't care to host the family holiday gathering anymore?

Now is a time for new ways of thinking and being. These new iterations do not have to be major turnarounds in your life. They may simply be tweaks but they work for you *now*, for who you are *now*, for your responsibilities *now*, for your pleasures *now*. A new you for this time in your life will allow you fresh fields of the mind, heart, and spirit to explore. You can learn new things just for the pleasure of learning them, knowing that you will not be tested afterwards. You can try a new way of interacting just because you want to, not because someone is making you do it "for your own good." As the adage says, you can wear red hats with purple dresses…because you want to.

And when you move on into the evening of your life, what you're discovering now may no longer work for you then because you will change even more as you add more days to your life. You will grow in new ways— ways that you can't imagine now. Do not live with fear about the now and the future. Life is to be enjoyed, *now*. Live it as fully as you can for who you are *now*.

Barbara developed an alternative persona. This was not kinky or evidence of a mental illness. She just decided to accept another "personality" into her consciousness. She even named this person Effie. Effie was a woman of the earth who loved to plant, maintain, and reap a large vegetable garden. Effie was a relatively free spirit, a true woman of nature. She wore loose fitting cotton dresses, often covered with a long apron and a large brim straw hat. Effie was not someone who lived connected to a computer, went to lots of meetings, and always thought about the appropriate attire for the occasion. Effie was not a talkative woman but when she spoke, people listened because Effie's words were comforting, kind, and insightful.

Effie did not appear very often, but the woman could call for her presence when she needed a reprieve from her life. Occasionally when shopping, the woman would look at an item and proclaim, "This is an Effie item! I'll buy it." As the woman aged, Effie became more of a companion and helped the woman move into this new way of living and thinking. Effie helped her let go of the morning of her life and move gracefully into the afternoon and evening.

Do you have an Effie in your life?

With love,
Your Secret Admirer

13

"Crying only a little bit/ is no use. You must cry/until your pillow is soaked!/Then you can get up and laugh/and splash-splash-splash!/Then you can throw open your window/and, "Ha, ha! ha ha!"/ And if people say, "Hey/What's going on up there?"/ "Ha, ha!" sing back, "Happiness/was hiding in the last tear!/I wept it! Ha ha!"

— *Galway Kinnell* —

Dear One,

Sometimes life stinks. You lose people, dreams, careers, health, and maybe even your faith. You were going along, minding your own business when wham, life changed in ways you did not want to welcome. Or maybe the loss crept up on you. You did not even realize that something or someone significant was slipping away. And then there it was: a huge hole in your heart, mind, or soul.

What to do? Do you tough it out? Use affirmations that everything is going to be okay? Say "It's God's will"? Crawl under the covers and not come out for days? Give yourself a week to grieve and then get "back to business"? Avoid your friends? Hold "it" together for everyone else, being strong?

Come on, get real. When you experience loss, you... EXPERIENCE LOSS! Life changes. What you assumed about today or tomorrow has just changed…maybe forever. You can tell yourself all kinds of stories about the loss. Your imagined stories can explain, deny, or push away the loss. Stories can help you think about the loss without being continually devastated by what has happened.

However, at first, you need to acknowledge this loss in your life. Feel the hole. Allow the pain in your heart to move into your head, too. Only you will know what this looks and feels like for you. And then cry. Cry and cry and cry until you've shed your last tear. And then…then…laugh. Because you allowed yourself to acknowledge and feel the pain of your loss, you will…eventually…discover joy once more.

Your life will never be the same again. That's a fact. That is not necessarily a negative reality. It just is. Your life has changed because something important to you is no longer part of you. You can decide how you want this newly designed life to be.

Paul in the Christian Bible wrote to people in Rome to help them with some of the issues they struggled with. He said: "Suffering produces endurance, and endurance produces character, and character produces hope" (Romans 5:3-4). He goes on to write that in hope, you find love.

In your last tear, you find love, joy, hope, and delight…all those things you thought were gone when you lost someone or something dear.

It is not easy. Even Paul started with suffering, pain, loss, and disorientation before he got to hope. The suffering eventually has to move to endurance. You begin to discover that you *will* get through today. You *will* get out of bed. You *will* eat a decent meal. You *will* acknowledge that even in the pain of loss that you are still breathing, your heart still beats, and your eyes still blink. You *will* endure and eventually you will know that you *will* get through this time.

You will notice that you are changing. Your character is deepening or widening. You notice others' pain in ways you had not before. You relate with compassion because you've walked a similar road. You begin to feel hope that you are indeed alive and that you will once again join the human race. Not in the way you were before…but you can see the possibility of life with hope and joy.

Dear One, cry until you've cried your last tear. Then laugh and join the lovely world that eagerly awaits you.

With love,
Your Secret Admirer

14

"It was as if I kept refusing to hear the voice that speaks from the very depth of my being and says, 'You are my Beloved, on you my favor rests.' That voice has always been there, but it seems that I was much more eager to listen to other, louder voices saying, 'Prove that you are worth something; do something relevant, spectacular or powerful, and then you will earn the love you so desire.' Meanwhile, the soft, gentle voice that speaks in the silence remained unheard or, at least, unconvincing."

— Henri Nouwen —

Dear One,

Who were you raised to be?

Yes, that is the question I'm asking: Who were you raised to be? What messages did your parents, teachers, friends, and ministers give to you?

Who were you raised to be?

Were you raised to doubt your own feelings or thoughts with comments such as "Don't feel that way" or "You don't really believe that!" Were you raised to be perfect with perfect grades, perfect manners, perfect hair, perfect language, and perfect teeth? Were you raised to be the family troublemaker or the "stupid" one? Maybe you were labeled as clumsy or super-religious or creative or overly-sensitive.

Who were you raised to be?

Whose career path did you follow? Your mother's? Your father's? Were you guided to become the musician your father wished he had become or the company leader your mother had dreamed of? Or maybe you wanted to be a stay-at-home mom because your own mother was never around. Did you want to be the first girl on your school's football team rather than regularly play bridge like your mom did?

Did you become a parent because your parents wanted to be grandparents? Did you marry the person your parents loved…more than you did? Or did you marry the person your parents hated because they disapproved?

Who were you raised to be?

You have many voices in your head. They have been important in making you who you are today. They have guided you and helped you make the decisions on which you stand now. And…and…and they have gotten in the way of your being able to hear that still small voice inside of you. You have ignored that inner voice because the other voices were powerful, often voices of people who loved you, who cared for you, and who wanted the best for you. Nevertheless, those external voices defined what was best for you—not your own internal voice.

Those voices, often spoken in love, thought they knew better than you what was best. And maybe for a time they were right. They *did* know what was best for you. But that was when you could not know these things for yourself. Now, you do. You know not to run into the street but to look both ways before crossing. You know not to touch a hot stove. You know that formal education is important in some ways. You also acknowledge that many of your important life lessons were not learned in a classroom.

You can decide which of these voices are still helpful to you and which you have outgrown.

Joan continued trying to be the perfect child her parents wanted even though she was now in her thirties. She watched her language, guarded her feelings, never voiced her own opinion, and showed up at her parents' house whenever they expected her to be there. She often wondered if she'd want to spend time with them if they weren't her parents.

After Joan married, she began trying to be the perfect wife for her husband. Unfortunately, being the perfect daughter and the perfect wife did not always align. After many starts and stops along the road to becoming who Joan knew herself to be, she decided to say, "To hell with them all," and she slowly, slowly, tiny step by tiny step, began listening to her own inner voice and following her own internal guidance system.

After some time, Joan discovered that her parents adjusted to her new strength and their relationship became surprisingly strong and healthy. Unfortunately, things did not work out so well for her marriage. But even that was okay. Her second husband loved the strong, independent, self-assured, and self-aware person Joan had blossomed into.

Letting go of all the messages you have gathered from bosses, family, friends, and even how-to books can be scary. Maybe that's why people choose to live as only shadows of their real selves.

You may wonder who you would be if you stopped listening to those outside voices. When you listen to your inner truth, you may feel threatened or scared. The messages from people who love you or have expectations of you may be security blankets. As someone who is trying to walk an uncharted journey, you are discovering that you have outgrown your need for a security blanket and you have other ways to feel secure… strengths and wisdom and knowledge you did not even know you had until you stopped letting others drown them out.

It's not always easy to create the safe space to allow your inner being to shine. It's mostly scary. And…it's worth it when you get through the scary parts of learning new ways of being. Just as a woman forgets much of the pain of childbirth when holding her newborn baby, you will forget much of the struggle of birthing your own, true self.

Take a chance, step out even in fear, listen to your inner voice that has been waiting for you to acknowledge its existence, and discover that joyous next step on your uncharted journey of life.

With love,
Your Secret Admirer

15

"If the Spirit of God never nudged us or made us uncomfortable, why would we ever let go of our old ways of doing things? How could we grow? God is simply calling you to a new kind of relationship."

— *Katherine DeGrow* —

Dear One,

Wouldn't it be lovely if things...when they are good... remained the same? It would be amazing to retain that 30-year-old body, but you still might want the wisdom and experience you've gained to this point. If marriages were always fulfilling, children always loving and obedient, and work always challenging and meaningful, wouldn't it be lovely?

Or would it? If you've never experienced cold weather, how can you appreciate warm...or vice versa? If you've never been lonely, how can you enjoy a good friend or two? If you've never had a bad cold, how would you know what breathing easily with no coughing, sneezing, or a sore throat feels like?

The truth is you want a life that is always enjoyable and easy. You want to be fulfilled and happy. When life begins to hurt, you may scream or holler. You may declare that life is not fair. Why should you have to deal with whatever is happening?

However, what if your speedometer got stuck in awful rather than pleasant? If the pendulum can swing to always positive, it can just as easily swing to always negative. Can you have one side of the pendulum without the other? Can you acknowledge that the good never lasts and that the bad doesn't last either?

Your favorite food is ice cream. If you had it every day with as many servings as you wanted (and it didn't add pounds to your middle), how soon do you think it would be before you craved something different? Perhaps a carrot?

Things change. That's simply the way life is.

And be honest…aren't you comfortable with many things of your life? Your family relationships? Your home? Your job? Your church family? Your weight? Your prejudices? Your identity? Why in the world would you change anything when everything seems to be going so well? The simple answer is that you wouldn't. You get comfortable in your niche. It's easier to stay than to leave. It's easier to hold on than to let go.

People often can't understand why a woman stays in an abusive relationship day after day, year after year. Part of the reluctance to leave a damaging situation is that she cannot imagine life any other way. She may believe that she deserves the abuse, that she is not worthy of being treated better. She may feel she cannot financially afford to leave. She fears he will kill her if she leaves. She may have to give up her home, her status, and her economic stability to escape. And so, she stays. She explains away her abusive situation until…until the beatings or verbal abuse become so bad for herself or her children that she must leave. The reality is that it may take her several tries before she can leave permanently.

You may have to hurt before you can release the way things are now. You may lose some mobility and then learn that there are a lot of kind people in the world who will reach out to help you when you are ready to accept the help. You may no longer be able to get out to visit others only to discover that people trust you when you call them on the telephone just to let them know you care and can listen. They know they can tell you their fears and hopes with full confidentiality. You may lose a job only to discover a long-hidden passion that you can now pursue. Or a better job comes along that you never would have hoped for. You may discover that having to be in bed to recuperate from an accident gives you the silent space to think about who you are and what you want out of life.

No matter what setback you experience, you may, with enough time, discover that the setback itself is a gift. It creates time and space for you to discover your next life lesson. Even when the setback brings anger or pain, you can eventually see it as a significant turning point in your life.

I suspect that you've heard people say that they would not wish the experience they'd gone through on their worst enemy but they would also not trade the experience for anything because of what it taught them. For example, many people with possible terminal illnesses report that they treasure each day, they value their time with friends and family, and they realize that things that used to matter to them no longer do.

When Janice graduated from seminary, she wanted to become the pastor of a congregation, but churches did not want a "woman preacher" in her small, rural area. Janice found other ways to minister to people by becoming a hospital chaplain.

She enjoyed her work immensely. She was asked to preach for ministerial colleagues when they went on vacation. Occasionally, she would teach a Bible class in a church. On very rare occasions, she officiated at weddings or baptisms.

She found small ways to work for short time periods in churches. Nevertheless, the dream of becoming a full-time parish minister never subsided. She felt unfulfilled and kept looking for the opportunity to pastor a church. Because Janice was struggling with general discontent with her life, she talked with a trusted counselor.

During one of their meetings, the counselor told Janice that as long as she kept looking over her shoulder at what she didn't have, she'd never see and enjoy what was right in front of her.

Janice was furious. That was not what she wanted to hear. She had wanted affirmation that she deserved to be a parish minister and was uncomfortable with what the counselor said.

As time went on, the counselor's words continued to haunt Janice. She began to find other ways to be involved with several congregations in new and creative ways while serving as a chaplain.

One day a church asked Janice if she would be willing to be their pastor. *Finally*, she thought. But then she thought some more and realized that she no longer wanted to be a parish minister. She saw that her experiences with congregations had revealed that she was not temperamentally matched for full-time parish ministry.

She had moved from holding tightly to what she thought she was *supposed* to do as a minister to claiming the ministry that had been truly hers all along. Once she let go of her assumptions, she no longer looked over her shoulder but eagerly embraced whatever opportunities were provided to her.

Today Joan is a chaplain with warm ties to a number of congregations. She gets to do all the things she loves doing with congregations—and none of the things she doesn't!

The moral of the story? Discomfort may be the very medicine you need to step faithfully into the wonderful journey that is ahead of you!

With love,
Your Secret Admirer

16

"A wise Hawaiian shaman once taught…a valuable lesson by saying '…All of the wisdom that I have to give you can be summed up in two words: Pay attention.' Pay attention and we evolve as we are meant to evolve. Pay attention and our loved ones receive the nurturing they desire. Pay attention and we are truly present in the moment. Pay attention and our hearts expand. Pay attention and God appears closer and mysteries become clearer."

— *Sue Patton Theole* —

Dear One,

Pay attention to your life and everything around you.

That is sometimes hard because you may see things as you've always seen them because…because…because that's just the way things are.

Suppose you had the opportunity to see life and the world and experiences around you through glasses of magnificent clarity. If you could truly pay attention without all the filters through which you have learned to view the world, amazing things might happen for you along this journey.

Imagine visiting a large room with bright daylight flooding through the windows. The floors are old heart pine boards. The only ornamentation hanging on white walls are masks.

There are hundreds of masks in this room. Some masks are the faces of old people. One visage looks like the model for an ad for senior citizens' cruises. Another is lined and well-worn. One's hair is well-coiffed, another's frizzy and straggly.

There are masks of men's faces, women's faces, children's faces. Masks that are European, African, Asian, Native American, and Middle Eastern. Masks of people who are homeless or very poor. Others with faces showing the benefits of money, good nutrition, and appropriate cosmetics.

There are masks for Presbyterians, Ba'hais, Baptists, Pentecostals, Catholics, New Agers, Unitarians, Mormons, Moslems, Methodists, Hindus and all other faiths. There are masks for straights, gays, and transgendered people, for educated and uneducated people, rich or poor; loved or battered.

You are required to wear whatever mask the attendant gives you—you have no choice. For the next thirty days, you will become whoever and whatever you believe a person behind the mask you're wearing would be.

If you had to step behind a mask vastly different from your own, live the realities of that person, and experience their feelings for an entire month, would your world be different afterword? Would you see the things that happen around you in a different way?

Most likely so. Once you see the world through another's eyes, you will open your heart to love and compassion in ways you cannot yet dream of. You will experience new vistas along your uncharted journey that you never experienced. You will see things you never noticed before.

With love,
Your Secret Admirer

17

"For I am convinced that neither death, nor life, nor angels, nor rulers, nor things present, nor things to come, nor powers, nor height, nor depth, nor anything else in all creation, will be able to separate us from the love of God in Christ Jesus our Lord."

— Romans 8:38 —

Dear One,

You are a person of faith. You can articulate that faith in ways that others embrace. You may hold your faith in ways that nourish your soul even when you have trouble finding a religious community.

You know that there is more to life than what is immediately evident. You have had experiences that are hard to describe— when life as you knew it stood still and something amazing grabbed you for even a second or two.

Maybe you have called yourself a Christian, a Jew, a Muslim, a pilgrim, an agnostic, and occasionally even an atheist. You have explored other faith systems. That's all part of your journey of faith and is okay.

You believe in God even though you're not always sure what to call Him/Her. Allah? Creator? Jesus? The Great Beyond? Higher Power? Mother? Father? Or you may be absolutely, one hundred percent, sure of your faith, your belief system, and your God.

Whatever you think about your faith or however you live out your faith, there is one thing that I remind you of. You are loved more than the person who loves you most in the world loves you.

No matter what is going on with you, you are held by this Mystery so tightly that you will never be abandoned. Nothing can separate you from this Loving Presence. There is no decision you can make, no action you can take, no mistake you can make that will pull you away from this holy and loving Mystery.

You may not always feel or know that you are being held close. You may even feel totally abandoned on this uncharted journey.

You have not been ignored or lost. You will find your way because there is a light in your innermost being that is tuned to something/someone greater than whatever is making you feel helpless, sad, or alone.

As you grew up, you may have had a faith that allowed no questions and tolerated no doubts. That time is past. You know that even though you continue to do the things you did as a younger person, praying and reading your Bible, you sometimes wonder what you are doing and why are you doing it. You scream, "If I was so good, so faithful, why do I feel so abandoned?"

Be assured that your quest is part of this transition time, of this uncharted journey. Many of your former ways of life and thinking no longer feel comfortable to you. They no longer provide the comfort they once did. That's okay. You are growing. You are letting go of things you have outgrown—from clothes to beliefs to relationships. You have experienced some loss. You are letting go. You are growing.

And, above all, nothing—absolutely nothing—can separate you from the Love, (that's love with a capital L) that created you, that placed you here on this earth, and that continues to sustain you in your journey.

This is your truth. Hold fast to it.

With Love,
Your Secret Admirer

18

"The fatal metaphor of progress, which means leaving things behind us, has utterly obscured the real idea of growth, which means leaving things *inside* us."
— *C.K. Chesterton* —

Dear One,

Sometimes as you make a transition from one way of being to another, you think that you must let everything go.

If you went through a divorce, you don't want to reclaim any of the positive things about the relationship because if you did, you think you would deny the inevitability of the split.

Maybe you've changed your religious perspectives. The ways you believed when you were a child no longer nurture your spirit. You believe that you need to get rid of some of those Sunday School songs you learned because now they seem childish.

Maybe you've found yourself needing to move from a large home to a small apartment and you've been forced to get rid of items that have meant so much to you in the past.

Now that you've made the move from old relationship to new, from old religious beliefs to new, from an old home to a new one, you feel bereft. You knew you *wanted* to walk away from all the old ways. You know you *needed* to walk away. And yet, you feel a big hole. You want to move on, but you just can't seem to let it all go.

You do not have to. Search inside yourself for what is meaningful from a former relationship. Did the pain you experienced teach you valuable lessons for your next relationship? Did you develop skills for coping that continue to be helpful? Did you have insights about yourself—positive and negative—that are essential for who you are today?

What is profound from the religious beliefs that you were raised with? Do you remember with fondness some of the people who taught you as a child? Did they plant the seeds of faith yearning in you? Did they give you the foundation that you were able to build on for your faith beliefs today? Do the old songs still speak in fundamental heart-ways that undergird your changing ways of understanding faith, God, and spirituality?

What was special about your old home? Even though you gave or threw away many, many things, you still have the memories. You still have your heart filled with the wonders that your former home nurtured. The things are not important. The relationships, the experiences, the stories embodied there are still hugging you.

There are other experiences, thoughts, and relationships that you leave behind on your uncharted journey. They are not lost. You keep the things that helped you grow to this point and you let all the rest go. Because of every experience in your life, good and bad, happy and sad, uplifting and downgrading, you are who you are today. Cherish the pearls of all this living and embrace the internal peace that these gifts bring you to today, now, in this time, in this place. You are special because you continue to grow and hold onto the essential pieces of who you are.

With love,
Your Secret Admirer

19

"Oh my God, what if you wake up some day, and you're 65, or 75, and you never got your memoir or novel written; or you didn't go swimming in warm pools and oceans all those years because your thighs were jiggly and you had a nice big comfortable tummy; or you were just so strung out on perfectionism and people-pleasing that you forgot to have a big juicy creative life, of imagination and radical silliness and staring off into space like when you were a kid? It's going to break your heart. Don't let this happen."

— Anne Lamott —

Dear One,

Don't you just love Anne Lamott? She says things in such an on-the-mark way!

A group of women met for coffee and they talked about some of the changes they were going through with their bodies and their families. They each were doing more of the things that gave them pleasure and had released those jobs that kept them tied to schedules every day. They fully enjoyed much of their lives and if you had seen them, you probably would have wanted to join their group because of the laughter and joy that exuded from them.

One of them said, "I don't mind people looking at the shape of my legs. It's just I don't want them looking at the old-looking skin on my legs!" All laughed and agreed with the comment.

Another said, "I don't care. I'll still wear shorts this summer—but, of course, not to my volunteer work!"

The first woman looked at the other woman's legs and decided that her skin was not much better than her own. Nevertheless, long pants would be her choice, no matter how hot it was outside.

Do you compare your legs, your voice, your skin, your weight, your rear end, or anything else to someone else and decide that you are lacking? Your skin is not as taut as the person's you are comparing yourself to. Your weight is distributed about your body in ways so that no one would think you were in your twenties. So, you decide not to do something you want to do because of what "they" may say.

How silly is that?

Yes, it's silly not to pursue an idea, a dream, a clothing style just because people may say you're old, you're not talented, you're fat/skinny/flabby.

So, what? So, What? SO, WHAT?

When are you going to be you? When are you going to realize that what other people think of you is none of *your* business? When are you going to be the fullest, most glorious, most wonderful you that you are?

How about now?

With love,
Your Secret Admirer

20

"We cannot always choose what we experience, but we can choose how we experience it."

— *Rev. Steve Garnas-Holmes* —

Dear One,

Some truths are so simple that we simply miss them.

"We cannot always choose what we experience, but we can choose how we experience it."

Billy, age five, tried to pour himself a glass of milk. The carton was bigger than he could handle, and milk spilled all over the kitchen floor. He was scared because his mom had told him to wait until she came into the kitchen and she would get his milk for him.

When his mom came into the room, Billy looked up at her, expecting for her to be angry with him. But rather than finding displeasure on her face, he was astounded to see a smile. His mom told him to take off his shoes and they "skated" in the milk on the floor.

When Billy grew up, the grown man he became knew that even spilled milk can be the basis of love, surprise, and unexpected joy.

The treasured family heirloom that breaks is only a thing. The person who broke it is the treasure, not the thing. You can grieve at the loss of something of sentiment—or even its value on Antiques Roadshow AND still embrace the individual who caused the accident. You can decide which is more important: the thing or the person.

You receive an unfavorable diagnosis. You can decide to begin your dying process immediately by withdrawing from life and relationships...or you can decide to live as fully as you can until you die. You can spew your anger about this reality or you can open your heart to those who want to support you.

You get turned down for a special job you wanted. You can blame the employer, your references, your age, your health, or whatever/whomever else you choose...or you can feel your feelings of disappointment and then eagerly look for the next door to open for you. You can look at the things that intrigued you about a denied opportunity and figure out ways to include those things in your life.

A relative says something or behaves in a way that disappoints you or hurts your feelings. You can decide to let her know exactly how you feel—strongly and unfiltered—or you can try to see her side of the situation and then calm down and decide to try to keep your heart open. At an appropriate time, you can share your feelings with her without demanding anything from her because all you desire is to keep love flowing between the two of you.

You see the latest photo taken of you and you cannot believe that the person in the photo is you! When you did get so wrinkly? When did your neck become a turkey neck? How did your high cheek bones end up in the middle of your face?

You can decide to hide now and forevermore. Another option is plastic surgery. You can try the latest "miracle" cosmetic. Or you can decide that your face shows you live and love life. You can embrace your looks even while deciding that photos will now only be taken from a certain angle! The choice is yours. So is whether you will keep that photo or cast it into the garbage!

Dear One, good and bad things will happen in your life. You will decide how you choose to think about them, what you want to do about them, and how you will proceed. Sometimes you will need to give yourself permission to rant and rave and shout and scream and laugh and cry for a brief time in the immediate aftermath. Once you deal with your animal brain reaction, you will always have a choice in what happens next.

With love,
Your Secret Admirer

21

"Everybody screams—and I include myself—'I can't do this and I can't do that!' and 'I used to do this and I used to do that!' and 'Baaah!' The lesson to be learnt is to understand the promotion from plum-easy doing to the surprisingly difficult non-activity of just being. Be patient, be gentle, be nothing. Somebody said that the real vocation of old age was to give out love."

— *Ronald Blythe* —

Dear One,

I have a list of words for you to lose from your vocabulary. They are: can't, perfect, but, should, and ought.

Can't. I can't keep your child for you. I can't lend you money. I can't fly on an airplane. I can't think positively. When someone says, "I can't," it is very easy for another person to come back with, "Well, you could if you wanted to."

"I can't" implies that you are powerless. You *could* keep a child IF you had the time or strength but obviously those things are out of your control. You *could* lend someone money, but you imply that you have no control over when and to whom you will lend money. If only you had that kind of control, then you would offer the loan. You *could* fly on an airplane if only you were in control of your fears.

When you say "I can't," you relinquish the power to make your own decisions. Better language is "I won't." I *won't* lend you money suggests that you are making a decision based on your own well-considered reasons. Perhaps you've loaned the requester money before and she did not pay you back. Maybe she mismanages her money or has addiction problems. *You* made the decision not to lend money to family or friends. Try substituting "I won't" whenever you begin to say, "I can't" and see what happens.

How about "perfect"? Imagine what might unfold if you dropped it from your vocabulary. What new doors would you be willing to walk through if you did not need to be perfect? If you did not need to look perfect? If you did not need to have perfect social skills? If you were not embarrassed because your eyes and ears and gait weren't as "perfect" as they used to be and you need adaptive aids to see, hear, or walk?

Possibly you would finally take those piano lessons that you've always wanted to attempt. Maybe you would wear a bikini. (Okay, maybe not, but who knows?) You could choose to go on a tour with people who are total strangers. You could try out for a drama troupe. You could go out without makeup. Oh, the amazing, wonderful things you could take advantage of if you gave up the concept of "perfect."

Then there's "but." The word "but" can be a very negative word. You may have used it in a sentence that begins with a positive statement: "I love what you've done with your hair *but* purple...really?" That's not much of a compliment, is it?

However, if you said, "I love how adventurous you are," while acknowledging *to yourself* that purple isn't a color you would have chosen, you have shown appreciation, without judging, for someone whose actions or desires or opinions don't match yours.

When you say, "I love you, *but* I wish you would come see me more," you place conditions on your love. Better to say, "I love you *and* I wish I could see you more." You have opened the door to love and to the very real wish that you could spend even more time with your beloved.

And, then there are the killers of your soul—the words "should" and "ought." Both play into the word "perfect." Perfect people live with a lot of *should*s and *ought*s. You may have been raised with many *shoulds (and should nots)* and *oughts*. As a child, you were told you should not get angry. You ought to obey your superiors. You should not do anything to embarrass your mother or father. You ought to always put others first. On and on.

You can substitute *should* with *could*. You may often say, "I should go see my mother today." Try switching your language to "I could go see my mother today…or if not today, then tomorrow or the next day." Using the word *could* rather than *should* can give you new insights into your choices for your life.

All these words—can't, perfect, but, should, and ought—are constricting. When you realize how using these words places unnecessary (and self-imposed) limitations on you, and how often you've let them influence both large and small decisions you've made, you can make a new decision: Will you continue to allow yourself to live with them?

Be gentle with yourself. You deserve it. Change your words and love who you are.

With love,
Your Secret Admirer

22

"In the world of sleepwalkers, intimacy is all too often replaced by anonymity. Many people let years pass without letting others know them deeply. They are just as homeless in their inner lives as people living in cardboard boxes on the street."

— *Frank MacEowen* —

Dear One,

Wake up! Wake up to life in its fullest. Wake up to the challenges, the joys, the frustrations, the fears, the thrills, the silence, the noise, the love, the hate, the desires, the dreams, the hidden things, the hurts, the strengths…all the things that are in you and surround you every moment.

As you read the things there are to wake up to, I imagine your heart began pounding. Your breathing became shallow. You may want to quit reading this letter. Am I right?

It is so much easier to keep hidden those deepest parts of yourself. You wonder if your friends and family would *like* you, much less *love* you, if you allowed some of the real you to come out and play. So…minute by minute, hour by hour, day by day, week by week, year by year, you've played a role. You've learned the lines given to you by other people.

You could qualify for an Oscar because you are so believable in your role. You've worked very hard at your performance.

It's not easy, is it?

If you received an Oscar, after all the applause, you'd probably come back home and wonder if you really want it, because you know it's really an award for being an imposter—someone you are not. You wonder if you rewrote the script you were given, put the drama/comedy into your own words and directed it yourself if anyone would be interested. Would anyone care?

Waking up, coming out of hiding is scary indeed... especially when you first begin. Then, gradually, you notice that you sleep better and enjoy life more. You give yourself permission to try new things, go new places, and think new thoughts. You decide to leave places, jobs, or people who do not appreciate the real you. You choose to say no...or yes...when that's what you truly want to say.

True-you. Maybe you could try for a day to meditate on your thoughts and actions to discern if they are true-you or not. If they are not true-you, you can decide if you want to try something new or continue, at least for a time, to keep this part of you hidden. But you will recognize, at least, when you are being true-you and when you are not.

True-you things do not have to be big and flashy unless, of course, that's who you really are.

George decided that one of his dreams was to sit in a restaurant, hear the music playing, jump up, grab his dining partner, and begin singing and dancing. He admires people who walk down sidewalks moving their bodies and singing to the music playing in their earbuds. He appreciates their lack of inhibition. He knows the true George is an impromptu performer but he's afraid that his children will decide that he is certainly sliding into dementia and will "lock him up." He's aware that there is "another person" living in him so he finds ways that feel a bit safer for him to leap into impromptu performing.

What does George do? He makes up funny songs and limericks in the privacy of his car or his home to entertain certain members of his family. He especially likes to drop his pants and waggle his naked bottom at his wife. She laughs. He laughs.

George's true-you moments nurture his soul and he maintains his propriety when it's important. He's comfortable in his life, knowing who he is, and yet making appropriate accommodations to society's expectations.

It's the not acknowledging who you are that strands you in an isolated, lonely land. In letting trusted friends and family see and embrace the true-you, you discover that you are no longer living unconnected. You are no longer alone. You can claim your rightful place in this world, whether "they" like it or not.

With love,
Your Secret Admirer

23

"The first half of life is discovering the script, and the second half is actually writing it and owning it."
— *Richard Rohr* —

Dear One,

Sometimes figuring out what's next can be a daunting task. So much has changed for you. Children no longer need you as they once did. Your body feels different to you. Your financial resources are different. The church and community responsibilities that you once enjoyed so much have lost some of their intrigue. Even your long-time neighbors moved to be closer to their children. Life has changed.

You now have choices. You can (1) moan and groan and wish for "the good ole days," (2) you can accept life is what it is now, or (3) you can move into this new stage with hopes and dreams. I suggest option #3.

As suggested by Jack Canfield and Mark Victor Hansen in their book *The Aladdin Factor,* write down 101 wishes. Write down everything you can think of that you wish for, big or small. This may take some time...maybe days or weeks.

Keep pushing yourself until you have all 101 wishes written down. Be a specific as you can. If you want a new car, list the model and color. If you want to learn a new skill, write exactly what skill you want to learn. For example, if you want to become a better cook, your wish might be to take a course in pastry baking at the local community college. If you want to read bestselling fiction as soon as it comes out, your wish might be to learn how to reserve books at the library. Every wish should be yours and one that you could envision in your wildest imagination. (But probably not that the television "hottie" will ask you out.)

All this is to say that you already know what kinds of things you would like to do—*if only*. You simply have to jump in. You might not know the fullness of what you have to offer. But you do know the next first step which will lead to the next first step which will lead to the next first step.

Yolanda decided to write down her 101 wishes. Even though she was in her mid-forties and carrying more weight than she desired, she wished to become a dancer. Yolanda enrolled in dance class and decided that she loved, loved, loved dancing. She even joined a dance troupe that performed in various community events. She never would have taken that first class if she had not written down her secret wish on her list.

Try it and you will discover ways to live further into the life you KNOW is there for you—that life you've known was inside you from the time you were a tiny child. The life you have wallpapered over many times is demanding now to be released.

Write your 101 wishes and begin living them!

With love,
Your Secret Admirer

24

"If you don't have the wound of a broken heart, how can you know you're alive? If you have no broken heart, how do you know who you are? Have been? Ever have been?"

— Edward Albee —

Dear One,

Life is hard. Things happen that you do not want. People disappoint you. Plans fail. Loved ones die. The world is in turmoil. Your beloved pet dies. Floods, hurricanes, and fires remind you how fragile life can be. Yes, life is hard.

Your heart breaks.

You hurt.

You wonder about the purpose of it all.

You question why you even care…about any of it.

You are in agony. This very pain is the place from which the next steps of your life begin. Because you hurt, you know you are human. You are not a machine. Machines don't hurt. You do. Remember this.

Your pain reminds you that you cared, you loved mightily, you invested yourself in something splendid. You know that you are alive even though you may wish you weren't in the midst of grief.

Sit with your pain and then give yourself permission to love yourself because of your pain. Love yourself because you know that you are not dead inside. Dead feels nothing. You feel everything! Love yourself because you discover strength that you did not know you had as you move through the brokenness.

Love yourself because you *did* care, love, and invest yourself. Love yourself because from the manure of this pain you will find rich soil in which to grow new dreams, new ways of loving, and new ways of being the wonderful human being that you are. Love yourself because you have experienced the pain of being human and you have survived! Now go out and discover more about the wonderful you that you are.

With love,
Your Secret Admirer

25

"Learn and obey the rules very well,
so you will know how to break them properly."'
— *Dali Lama* —

Dear One,

Matilda was a cook who knew how to throw a meal together
if all she had was a can of cream of mushroom soup, a pound of
ground beef, and some kind of canned vegetable on the pantry
shelf.

She called herself creative. If she needed cheese for a dish
but had none in the refrigerator, she grated some carrots. After
all, she thought, they were orange like cheddar cheese!

Matilda believed that her meals were always healthy and
nutritious. Other people might have disagreed, but she really
tried not to serve junk food. Her supreme dish that became the
talk of her family for years was a casserole made from canned
spinach, cream of mushroom soup, puffed rice cereal (for a bit
of crunch), and shredded carrots (no cheese that day).

Matilda knew that her sons needed the nutrients of this
meal and knew that if she told them they were having spinach
casserole, they would not take even a teaspoonful for their
plates. Therefore, Matilda told her children that they were

having Star Wars food for dinner. They ate the casserole (who wouldn't eat Star Wars food?) and loved it…until they asked what was in it.

After that, whenever Matilda put an unknown dish in front of her sons, one of them would ask, "This is not Star Wars food, is it?" After yet another "creative" dish had been placed on the table, one of her sons quipped, "Mom, you know that you really need to know HOW to cook before you begin messing with the recipes?"

That was Matilda's weakness. She had never really learned to cook. Both her mother and her grandmother were wonderful cooks so Matilda thought she didn't need to cook when growing up. Oh, her mom and grandmother tried to teach her, but Matilda preferred to be outside playing sports. She tolerated her grandmother's efforts to teach her how to make a peach cobbler but ran outside to play after putting the cobbler in the oven. Had her grandmother not been in the house, the cobbler would have burned and possibly taken the house with it!

Matilda managed to feed her husband and sons, but she was a utilitarian cook at best. Had Matilda taken the time to learn the basics of cooking beyond opening a can and dumping food in a bowl, pot, or pressure cooker and throwing in some spices, she could have become truly a creative cook. She had the instincts but not the skills.

That's the way life is. When you take the time, and make the effort to learn the traditions, the skills, the rules of anything, then you can break them in truly creative ways.

Knowing the rules and then deciding to move beyond them is an important skill. Choosing to break the rules for your own reasons is different from not knowing the rules in the first place. For example, when dining outdoors, you may choose to serve your guests with mason jars for beverages, bandanas for napkins, a shower curtain for the table cloth, and mismatched chairs around two planks set on saw horses. Your guests will admire your creativity as a host because they know they've also eaten at your formal dining table in a very different style. They know that you know the difference between mason jars and cut crystal and the experience is fun.

You may worship in a congregation that expands your mind and your faith beyond the basics you were taught as a child. You trust your minister because you know that she was thoroughly trained in doctrine, the Bible, and traditional worship and can move beyond those fundamentals to soul-stretching teaching, worship, and mission service.

Your medical professional, trained in traditional medicine, now incorporates complementary health options into his practice. He talks with you about nutrition alternatives to prescriptions and suggests acupuncture, massage, reflexology, or cranio-sacral therapy. He listens to you and determines with you the best protocols for possible end-of-life issues rather than pushing you to procedures that may cause your last days to be spent with tubes coming out of many places in your body and in isolation from friends and family. He knows how he was trained and with experience moves beyond some of those basic protocols as he treats you—a whole patient—rather than just a sick organ system.

Simply because you learned certain ways of thinking and doing does not mean that you cannot move beyond them. You can break the rules when you believe it is the right thing to do for who you are becoming. You have permission…from your innermost being…to move out of anything that is rigid and holds you back from the next steps on your uncharted journey.

Go ahead. Run barefooted before it is officially summer. Wear white after Labor Day. Eat hot dogs on Thanksgiving. Say no when you are expected to say yes.

Learn the rules and then break them!

With love,
Your Secret Admirer

26

"Anything that leaves you more fearful, more isolated, more
disconnected from other people, more full of judgment
or self-hatred, is not of God, does not follow the Rule of
Love—and you should stop doing it."

— *Mark Yaconelli* —

Dear One,

During times of transition, you tend to want to beat yourself
up. You tell yourself you have no friends, you are getting old,
no one loves you, you are losing your mind, you do not know
how you will get out of the bed in the morning, on and on.
Why do that to yourself?

I know, I know. If you could stop the negative roller coaster
in the amusement park of your mind, you would. When you are
unsure of what is next on your journey, it is hard to be upbeat,
unafraid, and hopeful.

Dear One, so many of the thoughts and plans you come up
with are dark and dangerous. You know in your rational mind
that you will get through this period in your life, and yet you
want to end this painful time. You begin thinking about all the
many ways you could stop feeling so useless—so like a blob of
chewing gum stuck to the bottom of your shoe, so alone.

Be patient with yourself. Some of the best words in the English language are "This too shall pass." Put one foot in front of another, even if you must shuffle along with your head hanging down. Hold on for this day. At the end of the day, breathe with relief that you made it through. Tomorrow will be better... or not—but you will have tomorrow.

When you are irrationally afraid, know that this is not your best you. This is not what the Creator of the World wants for you. When you feel disconnected from other people, remember that God is Love and love is part of relationships. The Creative Force of the World does not want you to be disconnected. When you hate yourself, remember that the Holy One of every religion on this earth knows you are a wonderful being.

It is sometimes hard to hold onto the concept that there is Something/Someone who surrounds you even in the midst of agony. You may scream that IF there were such a mysterious presence who loves you, then why...in God's name...does that Presence not come?

Screaming is okay. After you've done with your screaming, remember the Rule of Love. Love overcomes the irrational fear because you are not alone in that scary place. Love helps you reach out to another human being...the checkout person at the grocery store, the kid walking past your house, the woman you keep bumping into in the overcrowded aisles of the off-brand store. The Rule of Love leads you to open your hurting heart just enough to allow another's smile in to begin to thaw the chill. The Rule of Love indicates that you are lovable even when you know that you are disappointed in yourself. The Rule of Love surrounds you with hope and grace.

You will get through this transition time. Hold on to that thought with the assurance that some higher power, whatever name you call that One, loves you more than the person who loves you most in the entire world. Walk away from fear and loneliness and self-hatred into the Love that's there for you.

Thomas's grief over losing his parents within months of each other became intense at certain times of the calendar even years later. His birthday, his parents' birthdays, the anniversaries of their deaths, Father's Day, Mother's Day, and Christmas were some of those trigger moments. At times, Thomas could acknowledge the date and allow his feelings to surface momentarily and then life became sunny again. At other times, the grief felt as fresh as when they had first died. He ached all over—in his mind, his heart, and his body.

One May-June period was especially painful. During those two months, Thomas dealt with the anniversaries of his mother's birth and death as well as Mother's Day and his own birthday.

During the middle of May, Thomas's wife transplanted a gardenia bush that had come from his mother's yard before she moved into a healthcare center. This was the second move for the bush in Thomas's yard and his wife confessed that she did not know if the gardenia bush would make it this time. Many of its leaves had turned yellow and slowly began falling off. She even discussed with Thomas the possibility of pruning the shrub back in order to give the roots less bush to support. After discussion, they decided to wait until cooler weather.

The week before Thomas's birthday in late June, his wife called him to look out the window. On the very top branch of the gardenia bush was a pure white flower.

Thomas was at first speechless. Then he said, "My mom sent me a birthday present!"

Live with the Rule of Love and experience the small miracles of life that are yours to receive.

With love,
Your Secret Admirer

27

"[There are] four great themes that recur with new urgency in the last third of life: freedom, intimacy, meaning, and death."

— *Henry Simmons* —

Dear One,

Freedom, intimacy, meaning, and death. Do these words remind you of issues you are facing on your uncharted journey? If so, know that other people also ponder, yearn for clarity, and seek support for freedom, intimacy, meaning, and death.

Freedom: Do you have more—or less—freedom than you did a year ago? If your health is good and you have raised your children and changed the grinding responsibilities of a full-time career, you may feel more freedom. Your time is yours to plan. You no longer must arise every morning with the alarm clock. Even if you still wake at 6:00 a.m. as you have for years, you have more leisure because you do not have to hurry to leave the house at a certain time (unless you have an early yoga class!). You may have the freedom to pursue a long-held dream of a new career, travel, or stepping out of your definitions of yourself. You have the freedom to try on new ideas or expand old ones. You can spend time with family and friends, time that often had to be squeezed into the weekends earlier in your life.

If your health or finances have been challenged, you may have less freedom than you did a year ago. You may no longer feel comfortable driving at night. You may not be able to afford to eat out at "nice restaurants" as often as you once did. You may not be able to do many things as easily as you did a year ago.

Freedom becomes a constantly negotiated idea for you to ponder. Can you do this? Or not?

Intimacy is another consideration. Who do you share your fears, hopes, pain, and laughter with? Is your best friend still available to you? How many of the people who share your history are still around?

Francesca went through a traumatic divorce. But with the help of her friends, she made it through.

One friend, Harvey, a work colleague, offered a listening ear but would make Francesca mad when he asked her, "What business is it of yours what your ex thinks about you?" She'd become furious but later realized how profound that question was for her own health.

Louise was the listener who helped Francesca interpret some of her powerful dreams that happened in the aftermath of the dissolution of the marriage. She supported Francesca with gentleness from a profound depth of faith and offered sage advice as Francesca began dating again.

Ralph was like a trusted brother to Francesca. He took her out to lunch and dinner and included her in party invitations. He made her laugh.

Mary allowed Francesca to gripe, moan, and even cuss her ex-husband and often agreed with her! Emily confirmed Francesca's suspicions about some of her former husband's activities and loved her like a sister. She became the playmate who loved to laugh and shop. She expanded the way Francesca thought about reality and truth through introducing her to energy work such as Reiki and other alternative health practices.

All five of these friends, Harvey, Louise, Ralph, Mary, and Emily, who had shared a significant point in Francesca's life were no longer available to her. All five had died relatively young from unexpected illnesses.

Francesca felt bereft. She realized that she would have to intentionally cultivate new people as intimate friends by being an open friend and listener to others. By offering others what her friends had given her, she hoped that she would once again have people with whom to share a history, albeit a new one.

Of course, there are issues of physical intimacy: hugs, sex, or help with toileting and bathing. Only you know how much touching you need or are comfortable with.

When you live alone, you may crave the kind touch of another person or even a pet. Find people who like to hug, schedule a massage, or get a delicious pedicure. If sex makes you happy, go for it. If you and your partner need some help, talk with a medical professional. Find ways to find sexual pleasure that are safe and nourishing.

If you have gotten to the place where you need help getting to the toilet or bathing, you may find this much intimacy is uncomfortable, whether with a family member or a caregiver. This is something that just must happen. Understand that people love you or care for you and want to help you live as full a life as you possibly can.

When you were a baby, you delighted in getting your diapers changed, being bathed by a parent, and having your toes played with. You may find that you enjoy those basic pleasures again. You are NOT a baby but you can still enjoy the physical touches you experienced as one.

Meaning: You wonder about what your life means now, meant in the past, and will mean in the future. I have already written much about this to you. Just remember that your life has meaning. There is no one else in the entire world who is just like you. Doesn't that count for something? Relish your uniqueness. Seek ways to enlarge your very distinct way of living and being.

Death: Yes, here is the big subject. You will die. Everyone you know will die.

You can decide what kind of death you want. Learn as much as you can about the decisions you or your loved ones may have to make as you near the end of your life. There are resources that can help inform you about possibilities. Two that might help are *Being Mortal* by Atul Gawande and *Extreme Measures* by Dr. Jessica Nutik Zitter. Talk with your doctor and your spiritual leader. Discuss these matters with your family. Giving them as clear instructions as you can may be the best present you will ever give them.

The transitions of life are full of highs and lows, ups and downs, pleasures and disappointments. Relish each step along the way and celebrate at each milestone.

With love,
Your Secret Admirer

28

"COME TO THE EDGE." / *"No, we will fall."* / "COME
TO THE EDGE." / *"No, we will fall."* / They came to the
edge. / He pushed them, and they flew."

— *Appollinaire* —

Dear One,

I heard a speaker, whose name I no longer remember, ask
each person in the audience to shut his or her eyes. He gave us
a moment to settle into the silence that descended on the room
and to adjust to our darkness. Then he said, "Imagine you are
standing on the balcony outside a lovely room on the eighty-
seventh floor of an exquisite hotel. The view is spectacular.
Then you notice that the glass railing that you thought was at
the edge of the balcony turned out to be no railing at all. You
are on the eighty-seventh floor standing on a balcony that is
only four feet wide from the hotel wall. Now walk to the edge.
Let your toes hang off."

Even as I write this, my heart pounds and my palms are
sweaty. Did that happen to you when you read that? Why?

We are both perfectly safe. I'm sitting here writing to you
and I imagine you sitting in a comfortable chair in your home,
reading my letter while drinking a cup of peppermint tea.

You get scared from what you imagine. You know that you were not at the edge of a precipitous fall and yet, your body told you otherwise. You imagine horror and your body reacts as if what you imagined is real. You decide not to pursue your opportunities because your imagination puts you into scary and frightening scenarios. You turn around, screaming and crying, shouting "No Way!!!"

Let's try again. Close your eyes. "Imagine you are standing on the balcony outside a lovely room on the eighty-seventh floor of an exquisite hotel. The view is spectacular. Then you notice that the glass railing that you thought was at the edge of the balcony turned out to be no railing at all. You are on the eighty-seventh floor standing on a balcony that is only four feet wide from the hotel wall. Now walk to the edge. Let your toes hang off. As you stand there, you begin to smile. You discover that you have wings. You slide your feet closer and closer to the edge of the balcony floor. Your wings begin to unfold. You take flight!"

My *Dear One*, you have wings. Trust them and use them.

With love,
Your Secret Admirer

29

"Be patient toward all that is unresolved in your heart and
try to love the questions themselves...Live the questions
now. Perhaps you will then gradually, without noticing it,
live along some distant day into the answer."
— *Rainer Maria Rilke* —

Dear One,

Life can be confusing, can't it? You are filled with questions.
Who am I? Will my children be decent human beings? Does
going gluten-free really make a difference? Is God real? What
color tee shirt will I wear today? Am I supposed to be doing
something to save the world? Can I just sit in my yard, do
nothing, and that's okay? Am I a bad person for wishing that
my loved one who is suffering so much would die quietly
tonight? On and on the questions circulate.

Questions, questions, questions. Do you want your mind
to let go of turning the mental picture box around and around
and around? If you study the box from this angle, then this is
the answer to your question. Turn the box forty-five degrees
and look at the situation and the answer changes. It's rather
like the Rubik's Cube, which requires turning colored squares
around, up and down, back and forth, until all of one color
appears on a side.

When you mastered the process, you could easily arrange all six colors to their six sides. Or maybe you never figured out how do it. Questions can be like that. You can look up and down, back and forth until you simply quit trying and give up. Do you yearn for peace from your ever-moving mind?

Sitting with the questions is different. You allow the questions to float in your mind and in your life. You are aware that you have unanswered questions lingering around. Every so often, you may allow the question to move to the forefront of your mind. You notice it is there, acknowledge that you still have this unanswered question lingering about, and you move on, letting the question float away. You wait until that moment when the answer becomes amazingly apparent.

Some questions need time to vegetate in the recesses of your life. Like a seed, they need fertilized soil. You offer a great deal of that with the messes of your life! Questions need time in the dark as do seeds. You know the dark of no clear answers even when you really want them. Like a seed, questions need patience before they can push through the soil.

Questions may require the alignment of other people's ideas, desires, or wants before they can produce answers for you. Questions need warmth, just as seeds require light and sun. Holding the questions gently in the middle of your spirit is way of surrounding them with needed warmth. Live with the questions just as a gardener lives with the seed she planted in the soil. Then one day, you will notice a tender sprout pushing out of the ground. Your answer is coming. Hallelujah!

With love,
Your Secret Admirer

30

"The pain of leaving those you grow to love is only the prelude to understanding yourself and others."

— *Shirley MacLaine* —

Dear One,

Gussie's mother died. Gussie mourned the loss for herself as well as for her father. Her parents had been married forty-eight years. They were rarely apart. Gussie wondered how her father would cope with the loss of his beloved wife. He had been especially involved in the care of her mother during the last months of her life. What would he do now?

Gussie was surprised. Her father became different. He was certainly more relaxed. Gussie thought that finally getting a full night's sleep after so many nights of getting up with her mother helped her dad. But there was more than that.

Gussie struggled to define what was happening with her dad. He seemed...fuller. He laughed more than she ever remembered him laughing. He played golf with his buddies and even began wearing those gaudy old-man golfing clothes. He planted a huge garden and gave away most of the produce.

He began taking spontaneous day trips. He might show up at Gussie's house one day and say, "Let's go the mountains to get some apples." Or he'd appear at her door and announce that he was there to work in her yard.

Gussie was amazed by who her father was becoming after the death of her mother. She began to wonder where this man had been hiding all her life. She had liked him before but now he was delightful!

This can happen. When you lose a loved one, you may begin to pull some of his traits and characteristics that you admired into yourself. You remember her laugh when she spilled a bag of potato chips all over the floor. You remember how he could take each day as it came, no matter what happened. You remember how kind your aunt was to anyone with whom she came in contact…and you want to have some of that in you.

When you lose a loved one, you may decide that you can now move beyond limits that you and your beloved embraced. You can attend the Baptist church—which would have caused your atheist mother to have a heart attack. You can dye your hair orange and your grandmother will no longer roll her eyes. You can explore parts of yourself that you kept hidden out of respect for a loved one or from fear of what she might say.

When someone you love dies, you experience a hole in your being, but you just might discover that you have within yourself untapped traits, characteristics, dreams, and callings just waiting for you to pull them out to plug the hole. You will always know the hole is a patched one, but you may also discover that the patch makes the garment that is you even more beautiful.

With love,
Your Secret Admirer

31

"The old woman I shall become will be quite different from
the woman I am now. Another I is beginning."

— *George Sand* —

Dear One,

Do you know the old saying that the river you stick your
toe into today will never be the same again? The water keeps
moving and moving. Leaves floating on the surface rearrange
with each second of the flowing water. The rocks on the bottom
lose or gain a bit more moss or smoothness. The fish keep
swimming. The sun moves across the water, creating sparkles
or shadows. The river changes every moment. It will never be
the exact same river as it is right now.

That's the way life is, too. You change with every moment.
Now you may need to go to the bathroom. Shortly you will
not. Now you believe one thing, but you hear a comment from a
friend or someone on television and you begin rethinking your
belief. Now you have one freckle on your hand. Tomorrow...
who knows! Humans constantly shed skin and create new skin.
Your hair changes in length, color, thickness, and texture.

The jacket you loved last year now seems dowdy and frayed.
Your skirts are too long or too short. Your shoes no longer
have heels that take you to the stratosphere. Your favorite

purse looks like it was run over by a train. The earrings that you wore for every special occasion now hurt your ears.

People who are close to you change. Your closest confidante has troubles of her own right now and cannot be the support you have counted on for so long.

Your spouse and children get older and are different. When your kids were little, you could pull them onto your lap and soothe their troubles away. Now, you must trust that they can handle their own lives. You hope and pray that they will make good decisions—without your input or advice. That time in your relationship is past (unless, miracle of miracles, they ask!). Who you are today is not the person you will be tomorrow, next week, next month, or next year.

Sure, some things will remain. You may continue to believe in the same political system or in the God of your childhood or that life is fair. You may hold onto the dream that if you are good, then life will turn out well. You count on the illusion that you will have no pain nor will those you love. You hold on to the idea that you will always be happy if you just have the right attitude.

If you are lucky, however, you will have opportunities to revisit some of your long-held beliefs, judgments, and prejudices to determine if they still fit into your life now. Do they still make sense to you? Have you moved more to the left or the right of where you were just months ago? Have you learned to let go or are you still holding tight? Are you more moderate in your expectations of others or are you more demanding?

You are different now from who you used to be. Even if other people think you never change, you know that you have.

If you like the person you are growing into, great. If you do not, you still have the opportunity to try on some different ways of being, thinking, and doing. It will not always be easy but that's the joy and challenge of this uncharted journey that you are on!

With love,
Your Secret Admirer

32

"All around me, the aspen trees are shedding their dried golden leaves. I need to shed, to let go of what no longer is alive, to get bare enough to find the bones of what is important to me. I need to let go of the ways of knowing that have not, cannot, and will not take me where I want to go."

— *Dawna Markova* —

Dear One,

One of the saddest things about traveling this uncharted journey is coming to the end, only to wonder why you held on so tightly to things, people, situations, or mindsets that could have been released. In the letting go, you would have created an inner freedom to explore new opportunities, new ways of thinking, and new experiences.

It seems that human beings are afraid to let go of what has worked in the past. They get stuck in roles that they've outgrown. They cannot move away from relationships that are no longer mutually nurturing.

Molly has a friend that she's known almost her entire life. At one point, they were as close as sisters. Her friend is married and has children. She has an interesting and full life.

Molly moved away and has an equally full and interesting life. She is single and a successful woman working in a predominantly male field.

Molly and her old friend attempted to maintain contact for several years even through the many moves that Molly's work required. But things have changed. Both women have changed.

Molly's friend continues to make overtures to her through various social media contacts, but Molly rarely responds. She has other interests and feels she doesn't have time to respond.

The reality is that the two women have nothing in common anymore except for memories of their younger selves and the mutual friend who originally brought them together.

Molly knows that this relationship is no longer nurturing but cannot totally cut off her former friend. Yet, she feels guilty when she does not respond to messages. She feels as if she's dragging around some of the past that she's more than ready to release.

Henry intended to write the great American novel. He had some small pieces published in various magazines or literary journals but the novel? Well, it remained in his computer, partially finished. Henry continued to think of himself as a novelist even though he'd never completed such a work. When friends asked, he'd say that his work was continuing even though he secretly knew the last time he'd tried to write was months before. As long as Henry thought of himself as a novelist, he could not see what other creative outlets he had available to him.

Henry got so disgusted with his efforts to write, he decided to walk away from the project, but he did not tell his friends. To them, he was still the struggling writer.

Henry began shopping for vintage furniture and items that could be up-cycled. Just for fun, he tried putting unusual pieces together and installed them in his garden. Friends began to ask if he'd do the same for them. He now has a thriving landscape accessories business. He considers himself to be an artist.

He still writes small pieces every so often. He has a blog but in giving up his idea of becoming the great American novelist, an entire new world opened for him.

Dorothy always pictured the kind of grandmother she'd be. Her grandchildren would love to come to her house because she would always have homemade cookies, lots of crafts projects, and a host of activities and experiences planned to have fun. She pictured her grandchildren lauding her when they were grown because she had been the steadying influence and the primary cheerleader in their lives while they were growing up.

But, when Dorothy's grandchildren were born, she was able to attend the birth of only one. They lived miles away and she could not afford the plane ticket to get there when she got the call that a baby was on the way. As the grandchildren grew, other relatives were more present in their lives than Dorothy was because of proximity and flexible work schedules.

Dorothy's image of herself as a grandmother began to suffer greatly. She found herself counting the number of times the other grandparents got to spend with her grandchildren and she came up short. She worried and worried that her grandchildren would not know her and love her. She worried so much she made herself sick.

Dorothy went to the doctor and began crying as she tried to explain how she felt left out of her grandchildren's lives. She was not being the grandmother she always saw herself as.

Her doctor was very kind and understanding. She pointed out to Dorothy that right now the children were too little to even remember much of what happened around them. She encouraged Dorothy to keep working at being the best person she could be so that when the children were older, Dorothy would have an interesting life to share with them.

Dorothy thanked the doctor but still felt guilty. Gradually, however, she began to realize that she did not even want to be the kind of grandmother who attended every recital, soccer game, swim meet, or dramatic presentation. She was comfortable having a life of her own, not built around her grandchildren's lives and schedules.

She thoroughly enjoyed her limited time with her grandchildren and thought carefully about what activities they would do together to build memories. She focused on each child and, as they got older, began sharing her own world of work, commitments, and life passions with each child. Her relationship with her grandchildren blossomed as Dorothy found her own way of being a grandparent, not one that she "thought" was the right one.

Some ways of letting go are small as in deciding to wear pants to church rather than a dress, or to stop wearing makeup that makes you look older. (You realize this only afterwards!) You may decide that you are not required to have floors so clean that people could eat off them. Who eats off floors anyway?

Just as leaves fall off trees, everything changes. The flowers you thought were dead put forth showy blossoms after a series of rainy afternoons. The home you thought you would never leave suddenly seems too large and its upkeep prevents you from doing other things you might enjoy. Travelling? Taking classes? Meditating?

Family members are born...and die. Even your favorite television show that you scheduled your Thursday evening around ends. Be willing to let go and see what happens. Watch expectantly and eagerly for what's next in the unfilled space that you've now created.

With love,
Your Secret Admirer

33

"Losing our loved ones is the hardest thing we humans will ever have to go through. I think that's why the good Lord gave us a sense of humor. Because if we didn't have that, we would surely all die of grief, don't you think?"

— *Fannie Flagg* —

Dear One,

Sometimes you just have to laugh. When you open the bag of flour and it flies all over your face…when you forget that you put a new red sock in the washing machine with all your white underwear…when you walk out of the bathroom with toilet paper on your shoe or backside announcing to world where you've been…when you discover that you went to the grocery store and your zipper was down…when you learned that your parent's social filters had disappeared and you'd been accused of trying to kill him or her…when your grandchild says, "Let's take a picture every Mother's Day of you so we can see how many more wrinkles you have."

You just have to laugh. Otherwise, you'd cry!

You have a choice. You can laugh or fret or cry. The choice is yours. I suggest laughter. Your heart will be lighter and you'll certainly have more fun telling the story to your friends!

Will you choose to live life with a light heart or with a heavy one? The choice is yours.

Sometimes it takes a while to get to the light-hearted approach to an event. Grief, hurt, anger, or disappointment may be the only response you can make at first. Maybe later, after the initial brunt has passed, you can choose laughter.

Go with a slight smile at first. That may grow into a little giggle. Eventually, you'll give yourself permission to have a full-on laugh. And if you're very lucky, you'll laugh so hard that tears will come to your eyes.

Then you'll know that you can live with a light heart again. It may be a bit battered with some dents and scratches, but it's whole and no longer tethered to that solid rock of I-can't-believe-this-happened-to-me!

Everyone makes mistakes. Everyone feels pain. Everyone experiences grief. Face it, everyone looks stupid sometime in life. How you deal with those things makes you the person you are. Choose laughter and eventually, you'll like yourself even more.

With Love,
Your Secret Admirer

34

"My name is I Am." He paused. I waited. He continued. /
—When you live in the past, with its mistakes and regrets,
it is hard. I am not there. My name is not I Was. /—When
you live in the future, with its problems and fears, it is hard.
I am not there. My name is not I Will Be. /—When you live
in this moment, it is not hard. I am here. My name is I Am."

— Helen Mallicoat —

Dear One,

What will you do today? Not tomorrow? I don't want to
know what you did yesterday. I want to know about today.

What do you feel today? What do you dream today?

What do you hope today? What do you yearn for today?

What do you regret today? What will you learn today?

What are you grateful for today? What are you learning
about yourself today? What are you learning about the world
beyond what you can see, hear, touch, taste, and smell today?

What causes you to smile today?

Today, my precious one. Not yesterday. Not tomorrow.

Today. Live in this moment. You will never have another
one like it…ever.

With Love,
Your Secret Admirer

35

"At the age of 50, my mother vanished. "A woman becomes invisible in middle age," she said. I replied with sympathy. "You misunderstand," she explained. "It's liberating." For the first time since puberty, she said, "What I am on the outside is less of a distraction from who I am on the inside. Now, women trust me, men trust themselves around me, and every conversation can be purely, completely human."

— Kate Braestrup —

Dear One,

Many people do not want to be invisible. They want to be noticed. They love being in control. They like walking into a meeting and being greeted by people already there.

Some people even *thrive* on being visible. They color their hair purple, green, blue. They stick jewelry through their skin in various places on their body. They get tattoos to commemorate special events or people or "just because." They wear clothes that don't fit or things that are super-current or super out-of-date. They work out to keep bodies taut and youthful looking. They speak loudly or with vulgarity or with winning debate-team skills. They have opinions...lots of opinions. They find ways to draw attention to themselves.

None of these things are necessarily bad, mind you. You have done many of these things. (We will not discuss which ones!)

Once you get used to being visible, you can be shocked when you discover that you are no longer what you once were. You can continue to work at being visible. Plastic surgeons, designers of clothing and decor, and "how-to" mentors are ready to help you maintain your illusions.

And yet, there is value to becoming invisible. You can follow your own internal guidance system without checking with others first.

Do you want to wear only loose jeans and big shirts all the time? Do it. No one is looking. Do you want to say whatever your opinion is? Do it. Because you are invisible, many people will not care what you think. Do you want to let your true feelings out? Crying? Laughing? Sighing? Do it.

You're invisible. You can be truly authentic because you no longer are judged by others. They no longer see you.

I admit that you will have some trouble when you first realize that you are invisible. That's just one of those growing pains. Remember when you thought everyone looked at you in middle school because you were taller than your classmates? And then some of them shot up a foot over the summer and you were no longer the tallest person in the class? Then, you enjoyed just blending in.

That's what's happening now. You can blend in. You now have all kinds of freedom just to be whoever and whatever you want to be. Enjoy it. Let go of the illusion that you are the center of the universe. Just be you without having to meet someone else's idea of you. You are now invisible.

You can fly! Go for it.

With Love,
Your Secret Admirer

36

"A key challenge for many of us in living a fulfilling...
life is developing new sources of significance and
feelings of self-worth."

— *Jack Hansen and Jerry Haas* —

Dear One,

Any time you go through a transition, you may question the reality of the you *before* compared to the you *now*. That can be a hard time.

Annette, an executive in a nonprofit, knew that her organization had reached a point in its growth where it needed to make some changes if it was going to continue to be vital and effective. She knew that bringing in a consultant would help her, the staff, and the board of directors consider what might be needed as well as craft new directions or emphases.

Annette eagerly prepared for the consultant's visit by gathering all the information he requested. She shared her anticipations for positive outcomes with her closest staff members and the leaders of the board. She did everything she could think of to prepare everyone for this next stage in the organization's life.

The consultant spent several days with the organization, meeting with staff members individually and in small groups.

He talked with recipients of the organization's services as well as key donors. He met with the board leadership as well as with the executives of other organizations that worked cooperatively with Annette's nonprofit.

After his intense examination of the organization, the consultant allowed a couple of weeks to pass before sending his observations and initial recommendations. When Annette read the report, she was devastated.

Annette had asked the consultant to come when she did because she believed the organization was strong. Nothing was significantly wrong or unhealthy. Annette believed the time was perfect to consider what it would take to move to the next stages. The report burst through that illusion.

Even though he complimented the overall organization and its management, the consultant found weaknesses throughout the organization. He submitted a list of recommendations for consideration.

Annette's first reaction was to dismiss much of what he offered. But since the board of directors had authorized hiring the consultant and participated in his visit, Annette had to deliver the report in full to them.

Annette met with the board members and as they considered the consultant's report line by line, item by item, suggestion by suggestion, she often left the meetings in tears. She wondered what was so wrong with how things had been. Why couldn't they keep doing what they'd been doing as they'd been doing it and simply add more to it? She struggled to let go of the old way of looking at and operating the organization.

Eventually as the recommendations were considered and the board of directors decided which to implement, which to tweak, and which to ignore, Annette began to discover the significance and wisdom of the entire process. She thrived in the newly-focused and energized organization.

That's how any transition can be. You can be thrust into a life change that you were not prepared for. Even if you knew the transition was coming—a child starting school, a child leaving home, retirement, parents becoming dependent on you, marriage beginning or ending—you find yourself questioning what was so wrong with before.

Why did things have to change? Why are you forced to redefine yourself now as a mother of a school-aged child and not a toddler, as an empty nester rather than a highly active and supportive parent, as a person with a non-schedule rather than a working professional, as an adult who must make life decisions about the needs of parents, as a married person, or as a single person?

Finding significance in your new role is certainly a journey. You are lucky when you can find someone else who is just a few steps ahead of you on this road. This person can commiserate with you, offer helpful tips, or laugh with you.

You can moan and groan about what you've had to let go of or you can decide that this next stage of your life has something to offer, challenges to relish, new friendships to cherish, and new ways to talk about yourself.

So what if you're no longer who you once were? You can decide how to define who you are now. In the past, you may have thought of yourself as a college professor. Now you are a writer, community activist, leader in your neighborhood, budding drummer, runner, caregiver, volunteer, reader of all the great classics, active grandparent, artist, meditator, gardener, Bible study group member, authority on the brown recluse spider, adult learner, sitter-on-the-porch so people can drop by, or anyone else you decide to be.

You will not always find it easy to find new significance or new feelings of self-worth, but when you do, when you are willing to take the next steps on this uncharted journey, you will be glad...most of the time...that you did.

With Love,
Your Secret Admirer

37

"So teach us to count our days
that we may gain a wise heart."

— Psalm 90:12 —

Dear One,

The poet of the Book of Psalms in the Hebrew Scriptures, a.k.a. the Old Testament in Christian circles, was a very wise person. Many of the 150 psalms are credited to King David, considered in Jewish history to be the greatest king that ever lived. Some psalms were written by others, possibly even a few by women! The imagery of the psalms can speak to the heart, no matter what faith a person may claim, if any.

One way to unleash the beauty and wisdom and harsh honesty of the Psalms is to read the same psalm for a week: Monday, Tuesday, Wednesday, Thursday, Friday, and Saturday. You may be amazed to read a phrase on Thursday that you'd already read every day that week and suddenly something astounding jumps out at you and captures your heart and imagination. By simply reading, day in and day out, you may begin to realize how pertinent the Psalms are for you...today.

Psalm 90 can be such an "aha" moment. *Count your days to gain a wise heart.*

Do you remember when you were a child and you eagerly anticipated Christmas? Beginning the first week of December you began marking the calendar to count down to the 25th.

You also tried to be a good child so that Santa Claus would not punish you with a lump of coal in your stocking. You marked your days and you paid attention—to your behavior, to the whispers of the adults, to the smells coming from the kitchen, and to the packages secretly coming into the house. You were diligent in thinking about each day, connecting with each person in your house, and eagerly anticipating what was to come.

When the psalmist suggests that you count your days, you can remember the December countdown to Christmas. When you are mindful of life with all its nitty, gritty, and goofy details, you will gain wisdom. Paying attention means staying engaged, not hiding in anger, "poor me" feelings, or drowning in despair...even though those things will happen. Paying attention is a challenge to embrace in order to live the life that you want to live.

When you pay attention, you will indeed gain wisdom. You'll be in touch with yourself...the best source to discover your own deeply held truths, beliefs, illusions, and realities. You may even discover wonders that astound you!

With Love,
Your Secret Admirer

38

"Many of us will go to our graves blaming others for the
conditions of our lives. We will do anything to avoid taking
responsibility for our part in our dramas. But making
others wrong and holding on to the pain of our past means
committing ourselves to a lifetime of limitation and misery.
And as long as we are blaming others for our circumstances
we have no freedom, because our resentment keeps us bound
to the very people –and the very circumstances—we dislike.
As long as we carry that seed of resentment in our hearts we
will have to create some kind of pain, drama, or discontent
in our lives in order to keep our blame alive."

— Debbie Ford —

Dear One,

Do you ever play the "If-only" game? If only my parents
had not fought so much, if only my spouse had treated me
better, if only my boss had noticed my good work, if only I
had not run that red light, if only…, if only. Yes, your parents
fought a lot. Yes, your spouse treated you terribly. Yes, your
boss did not pay attention to you, a very good employee. Yes,
you ran a red light and caused an accident. Yes, these and other
things, maybe even more awful, happened to you or because of
you. Do they define you today?

I repeat. Do they define you today? Only if you let them.

Roger and Margaret married and after a time, Roger began having personal issues that affected his behavior with his wife and his children. He became physically, emotionally, and verbally abusive. He controlled the family with rage—followed by periods of delightful interactions. The family learned to squelch words, activities, and opinions that might trigger a ranting tirade from Roger.

Eventually, the marriage dissolved.

Margaret determined to build a new and healthy life for herself. However, when she did something that in the past triggered one of Roger's violent assault, she would stop because she knew what he would say. She avoided some of the same things she had avoided in the past because that's what she had learned to do while in the marriage. She would hear Roger's voice saying in her head, "You think you're so perfect." "You never have time for me." "You're a controlling bitch." His words continued to affect how she behaved and how she thought about herself.

Margaret struggled with the poor self-image that had developed during her marriage to Roger. If only she had not married the man. If only she had not been so young. If only she had understood more about the issues that would surface in his life. If only she had been able to stand up for herself. If only.

One day, as she was about to go out with a new group of friends, Margaret put on new clothes that she bought especially for the gathering. As soon as she slipped the blouse over her head, she heard Roger's voice, his assessment of her outfit, and even what he would say about each of her friends.

And then it hit her. *Roger WAS NOT in the room.* The voice she was hearing was her own. She had continued to allow Roger to rule her life, even though he was not present and had moved on to other relationships and even to another community. She was living as a victim and she was doing it to herself.

Margaret decided that she no longer would give Roger real estate in her mind and heart. Occasionally, he still tried to move back into her head, but she decided then and there that she would no longer be his victim. She could be affected by Roger's destructive influences only if she allowed herself to be occupied that way.

People may truly be hurt in dreadful ways by other people. After a time for healing, each person has the choice to decide if and how long an incident or former way of life will continue to define him or her.

Will you be a rape victim or a rape survivor? Will you be child who was neglected or an adult who has discovered ways to nurture that wounded child and be a loving, caring, mature, and healthy adult? Will you be the younger person who made a bad mistake, or will you be a person who learned some tough lessons and now can move on with the past no longer defining you?

You along with everyone else have had some bad things to happen to you. You can learn from them, you can let them go, or you can lug them around. The choice is yours.

Dear One, if you find that you're having trouble taking off the victim role, please talk with someone who can help you find your way to new definitions of yourself.

With love,
Your Secret Admirer

39

"It is better to be disliked for who you are than to be liked
for who you are not—the only thing you really have to share
with any one, anyway, is your own state of being."

— *Judith Ann Parsons* —

Dear One,

Do you remember when you tried so hard to be liked?
Maybe it was when you were in high school. Did you listen to
the music that "everyone" listened to? Did you wear your hair
like the others? What about your clothes? How did all that work
out for you? Looking back on all that now, does it really matter?

Or what about when you were a young adult? What groups
did you join because you thought that would help you in your
career or your reputation as a parent or because that was what
people like you did?

Throughout your adult years, did you speak what you really
thought? Or did you keep your thoughts silent because to say
what you really wanted to say might ostracize you from the
group? Did you pretend to be someone you thought you needed
to be...for prestige, for lack of discord, for getting ahead?

If someone were writing your biography today, what
distinctive aspects about your life would they describe about
you? What made you stand out? Did you do anything that set
you apart, that showed the world how special you are?

Answering these questions is very important for you to move ahead. Who do you really want to be? Yourself? Or do you want to be the person your spouse, friends, children, or community want you to be? Maybe you've created an image of yourself to keep you from noticing even in your inmost being that you are not who you project yourself to be.

Why? Why in the world do you want to be someone other than who you are created to be? Why do you allow yourself to not accept yourself, the most precious gift you have ever been given?

So what if others do not like the freed-up you? Don't you get tired of maintaining your carefully-crafted image? Wouldn't you rather stand up, throw your chest out, hold your chin high, and shout, "Look out world. This is ME! This is who I am. Take it or leave it. I don't care because I LIKE who I am. If you don't like it well, that's a loss to you because I have my own thoughts, my own beliefs, my own likes, my own passions, my own faults, my own tastes, and my own perceptions. This is ME, and I'm glad of it!"

With love,
Your Secret Admirer

40

"It's the gift of limitations that frees us to find our own dream."

— *Mark Nepo* —

Dear One,

We all have real limitations—in health, social relationships, financial circumstances. For example, if you're not tall, you realized that you would never become a professional basketball player even though you loved the game. You discovered you had many other options for pursuing that passion and dream. You realized you could be a coach, a game announcer, a facilities manager, a designer of uniforms, a trainer, a sports medicine doctor. The limitations of height certainly closed one opportunity but provided many others.

That's what can happen in life. When you can accept and embrace your own limitations…and you DO have limitations… you can begin to explore other ways you can fulfill your dreams.

Eunice was a self-described people person. Everything she had done professionally involved active exchanges with other people. She had worked as a sales person in the home repair industry. She later went back to school and became a teacher. When she retired, she delivered Meals on Wheels and became a literacy tutor. All her life she laughed, talked, and interacted with others. Her ready laugh and willingness to listen made her a favorite person to be with.

Eunice's health deteriorated, and she ended up spending most of her days lying in a bed in a health care facility. When she was not in bed, she was in the bathroom or at a medical appointment. Her sphere of people became very limited.

Many people would have closed in on themselves, turned their faces to the wall, complained to anyone who came into the room, or begged to die. But not Eunice!

Eunice decided that she had the perfect opportunity to brighten the day of people who worked in very stressful jobs. She could listen to her care providers as they talked about their worries about their families. She celebrated with them the successes of their children. She could smile and always let her caregivers know how much she appreciated the care they gave her. She became a consistent positive influence on the medical personnel who came into her room.

She also decided that whenever someone visited her from her church, she could make the visit as meaningful to them as it was to her. She offered to pray for them rather than always seeking their prayers. Her friends and family enjoyed their time with her because she truly focused on them, their concerns, their fears, and their joys. Eunice decided that staying in a health care bed was just a new venue for interacting with people.

Embrace your limitations. Let them instruct you and guide you to the next steps on your uncharted journey.

With love,
Your Secret Admirer

41

"The difficulty lies not so much in developing new ideas as
in escaping from old ones."
— *John Maynard Keynes* —

Dear One,

Joyce went to a training workshop on leadership. In one of
the sessions, her small group was told that a company had rolls
and rolls of the kind of paper used to make tea bags. Since the
company did not package teas, it needed help trying to figure
out how profitably to use the paper. Joyce's group was assigned
the task of coming up with as many ways as possible to use the
papers.

The group began trying out ideas. One suggestion was
to turn the paper into coffee filters. Ideas flowed but most
continued to use the paper in a food-related way.

The trainers then told the group to take a break. They
were encouraged to walk around the training center's grounds.
During the break, they could eat some of the healthy snacks
provided. They could look at the beautiful handwoven tapestries
hanging on the walls. They could do whatever each wanted to
do during the break.

After twenty minutes, they came back together to continue
to work on their assignment. They were surprised at how

quickly new ideas came. The paper could be used in landscaping projects. It could be repackaged for art projects. On and on the ideas flowed.

When all the groups came together to share their projects, they discovered that their assigned tasks were not important. The purpose of the assignment had been to demonstrate the power of a leisure break when trying to problem-solve or to be creative.

Even while Joyce and her group were thinking about the beauty of their surroundings as they strolled the well-manicured paths or perused the intricacies of the tapestries, their inner minds were still working on the problem. The "play break" helped them to be more creative and productive.

Take "play breaks" along your uncharted journey. Here's a suggestion—put your mind to work writing seven syllable phrases. Here are a couple of examples:

It's-o-kay-I'm-not-per-fect.
It's okay. I'm not perfect!

O-LORD-be-with-me-to-day.
O LORD, be with me today.

Or, write some very bad haiku (first line has 5 syllables, second has seven, the third as five) such as:

Letting go is hard
But…it opens space for growth
Guess I'll decide yes.

I really want growth
God, I need you with me, right?
You're already here!

I know. Writing phrases and haikus may not be your idea of a break.

Find something else that takes you out of your present angst. Play with ideas, with a ball, or while baking. Do something that takes your mind off your current focus. Go for a walk or a bike ride. Let your mind and body play.

Then when you come back to whatever you are puzzling over, you'll be ready with fresh insights.

It works. Try it.

With love,
Your Secret Admirer

42

"Let me hear of your steadfast love in the morning,
for in you I put my trust. Teach the way I should go,
for to you I lift up my soul."

— Psalm 143:8 —

Dear One,

It can be comforting to know that someone else has been through or is going through what you are dealing with. Here is a responsive reading based on Psalm 143 that was written by a woman when her husband was dealing with significant medical problems. I hope it will help you.

Hear my prayer, O Lord; give ear to my supplications in your faithfulness; answer me in your righteousness.

O Lord, I am distraught. I'm turning to you because I know of nowhere else I can find comfort.

Do not enter into judgment with your servant, for no one living is righteous before you.

Please, God, do not abandon me at this time in my life. I need you now more than I have ever needed you before. I feel like everywhere I turn, there is no one who can love me and understand me as deeply as I yearn to be loved. I throw myself to you.

For the enemy has pursued me, crushing my life to the ground, making me sit in darkness like those long dead.

The enemy is so real. It has three heads: grief, fear, and loss of control. My spouse with whom I've lived and loved for more years than most can imagine is slipping away from me in both body and mind. I fear I will outlive my resources. I fear that I may have to give up my home I love. I fear that I will always feel lonely and ill of body and spirit. I'm losing control as my children step in to make more decisions, as the healthcare providers make decisions for me and my spouse, and as finances may force decisions I do not want to make. This three-headed enemy is indeed crushing my life to the ground. The world is very dark right now. I can scarcely breathe.

Therefore, my spirit faints within me; my heart within me is appalled.

Most Loving God, I just want to run away. I have no energy. I am overwhelmed with all the changes that are coming at me so fast. I cannot stand.

I remember the days of old, I think about all your deeds, I meditate on the works of your hands.

Sweet Savior, you have so richly blessed my family and our lives. I remember all the wonderful things you have offered to us. We have lived long and even in our struggles you have been there. I think back on my life, knowing the joys are greater than the struggles. You have surrounded me and mine with your steadfast love.

I stretch out my hands to you; my soul thirsts for you like a parched land.

I need you, my God. Without you, I cannot stand this life. Only you can give me strength to endure my enemies. I yearn to experience your closeness. I crave your loving presence.

Answer me quickly, O Lord; my spirit fails. Do not hide your face from me, or I shall be like those who go down to the Pit.

O Lord, my spirit truly fails. I am desperate to feel your presence. I feel as if I am living in hell, apart from you. Come, sweet Jesus, and let me know your love.

Let me hear of your steadfast love in the morning, for in you I put my trust.

Dearest Lord, you know that I'm not a morning person. When I open my eyes after an evening of seeking sleep, let me know once again your promises to always be with me. Renew my trust when my enemies try to erode my confidence in your abiding care. Give me hope that allows me to arise and face another day before my enemy.

Teach me the way I should go, for to you I lift up my soul.

Guide me, uphold me, lead me, prod me, sustain me, encourage me, and give me the peace of your faithfulness and love. My soul yearns for you.

Save me, O Lord, from my enemies; I have fled to you for refuge.

O Lord, the three-headed enemy of grief, fear, and loss of control is so powerful at times. Hide me under your wings so the enemy can pass me by without doing too much harm to me. Keep me safe so I can be strong even when under siege.

Teach me to do your will, for you are my God.

My God, I am your child. Help me to listen to your still, small voice when the enemy is roaring. Teach me what you would have me to learn at this stage in my life. This journey is not easy, O Lord. Teach me how to travel this road.

Let your good spirit lead me on a level path.

I want a level path, not the one that now feels like it is full of twists and turns, hills and valley, rocks and ruts. Give me a level path. Is that too much to ask?

For your name's sake, O Lord, preserve my life.

My life feels threatened from within and without. Preserve me so I can continue this path on which you have set me. Help me be loving to my dear spouse and to all those who cross my path. Be with me so that all will know that you are my God and I am your child.

In your righteousness bring me out of trouble.

Whatever happens, let me know that I live in your righteous plan. Help me to know that even the struggles of life are part of your path for me. Let me know that you will bring me out of trouble, even when it does not feel that way. Help me to feel deep in my soul the wonder of resurrection living after the crucifying moments of life.

In your steadfast love cut off my enemies, and destroy all my adversaries, for I am your servant.

I always want to be your servant. Let the enemy not take that away from me. Amen and Amen.

With love,
Your Secret Admirer

43

Dear One,

You most likely have been wondering who your secret admirer is. It's…YOU! Everything in these letters are ideas and truths already hidden in you.

So now that you know who your Secret Admirer is, you can switch your language to *me, my,* and *I.*

I am discovering my own truths. I will acknowledge them. I am finding my inner wisdom. I will follow it. I am hearing that small, still voice that is deep in my spirit. I will listen well.

I will let the world see, hear, and experience the wonderful me that is ME.

I can learn to trust my own best instincts.

I will lean on God, Allah, the Ultimate Reality, whatever name I give to the Truth That is Beyond All Truth. I will love richly because I am so loved.

Each transition in life is an opportunity to discover more about who I am, to find my strength, and to summon my courage. I will emerge from these opportunities when I choose to hang on, walk through the dark, and learn whatever lessons await me. It will not be easy, but I *can* and *will* do it.

This uncharted journey is a glorious adventure. I will embrace it!

With love,
My Secret Admirer,
Best Friend,
Biggest Cheerleader,
Deepest Listener, and
Wisest Guide

Me!

Endnotes

1. Henri Nouwen and Walter J. Gaffney. *Aging: The Fulfillment of Life* (Garden City, NY: Image Books, a division of Doubleday & Company, 1974) 13-14.

2. Reba Riley, *Post-Traumatic Church Syndrome* (New York: Howard Books, 2015), 335.

3. Albert Einstein quoted in Sue Patton Theole, *Freedoms After 50* (Berkeley CA: Conari Pres: 1998), 7.

4. *Each Day a New Beginning*, Hazelden Meditation Series (Harper/ Hazelden, 1982), March 24.

5. Rachel Naomi Remen, *My Grandfather's Blessings* (New York: Riverhead Books, 2000), 29.

6. Elizabeth Watson, Epigraph quoted in Irene Allen, *Quaker Indictment* (New York: St. Martin's Press,1998),1 quoted in Rochelle Melander, *A Generous Presence: Spiritual Leadership and the Art of Coaching*, (Herndon, VA: The Alban Institute, 2006), 125.

7. Frederick Buechner, *The Clown in the Belfry* (San Francisco: HarperSanFrancisco, 1992), 84-85.

8. Chinese saying, quoted by Helen Nearing in *Loving and Leaving the Good Life* which was quoted in Mary Pipher, *Another Country: Navigating the Emotional Terrain of Our Elders* (New York: Riverhead Books, 1999), 243.

9. Madeleine L'Engle, *Walking on Water: Reflections on Faith and Art* (New York: Bantam Books, 1980), 13 quoted in Rochelle Melander, *A Generous Presence: Spiritual Leadership and the Art of Coaching*, (Herndon, VA: The Alban Institute, 2006), 303.

10. William Butler Yeats, quoted in Tim Stafford, *As Our Years Increase: Loving, Caring, Preparing for Life Past 65* (New York: Harper Paperbacks, 1989), 87.

11. Psalm 31: 9-13 NRSV, New Revised Version of the Bible, copyright 1989 by the Division of Christian Education of the National Council of Churches of Christ in the United States of America. Used by Permission. All rights reserved.

12. Carl Jung, *The Collected Works, 20 vols.*, Trans. R.F.C.Hull (Princeton: Princeton University Press, 1973), Vol. 8, para. 787 quoted in James Hollis, *Finding Meaning in the Second Half of Life*, (New York: Gotham Books, 2005), 151.

13. Galway Kinnell, "Crying," *Three Books* (Houghton Mifflin Harcourt, 1993) appeared in *Spirituality and Health*, Jan./Feb. 2014.

14. Henri Nouwen, *Life of the Beloved* (New York: Crossroad, 1992), 28-29 quoted in Linda Douty, *How Can I Let Go If I Don't Know I'm Holding On?* (Harrisburg, PA: Morehouse Publishing 2005), 21

15. Katherine DeGrow quoted in Linda Douty, *How Can I Let Go If I Don't Know I'm Holding On?* (Harrisburg: Morehouse Publishing, 2005),18.

16. A wise Hawaiian Shaman quoted in Sue Patton Theole, *Freedoms After 50* (Berkeley CA: Conari Press: 1998), 55.

17. Romans 8:38 NRSV, New Revised Standard Version of the Bible, copyright 1989 by the Division of Christian Education of the National Council of Churches of Christ in the United States of America. Used by Permission. All rights reserved.

18. G. K. Chesterton, quoted in Mary Pipher, *Another Country: Navigating the Emotional Terrain of Our Elders* (New York: Riverhead Books, 1999), 130.

19. Anne Lamott, *Bird by Bird: Some Instructions on Writing and Life*. This quote is found in various places on the internet.

20. Rev. Steve Garnas-Holmes, *One Light Unfolding*, a newsletter quoted in Linda Douty, *How Can I Let Go If I Don't Know I'm Holding On?* (Harrisburg: Morehouse Publishing, 2005),132.

21. Tim Stafford, *As Our Years Increase: Loving, Caring, Preparing for Life Past 65*, New York: HarperPaperbacks, 1991, p 89. Stafford references Ronald Blythe as "another aging Christian writer."

22. Frank MacEowen, *The Mist-Filled Path*, xxii quoted in Richard L. Morgan, *Settling In: My First Year in a Retirement Community* (Nashville: Upper Room Books, 2006), 113.

23. Richard Rohr, *Falling Upward: A Spirituality for the Two Halves of Life* (San Francisco: Jossey- Bass, 2011), ix.

24. Edward Albee, The Play About Baby, quoted in Lama Surya Das, *Letting Go of the Person You Used to Be: Lessons on Change, Loss, and Spiritual Transformation* (New York: Broadway Books, 2003), 180.

25. Dali Lama quoted in Richard Rohr, *Falling Upward: A Spirituality for the Two Halves of Life* (San Francisco: Jossey- Bass, 2011), xxvii.

26. Mark Yaconelli as told by Anne Lamott in *Hallelujah Anyway: Rediscovering Mercy* (New York: Riverhead Books, 2017), 108.

27. Henry Simmons, *Soulful Aging: Ministries through the Stages of Adulthood*, co-authored by Jane Wilson, wrote the Introduction of and was referred to in the Preface by Richard L. Morgan, *Settling In: My First Year in a Retirement Community* (Nashville: Upper Room Books, 2006), 16.

28. Appollinaire quoted by Ernest Kurtz and Katherine Ketcham, *The Spirituality of Imperfection* (New York: Bantam, 1992. 163.

29. Rainer Maria Rilke, *Letters to a Young Poet*, trans. M.D. Herter (New York: Norton, 1993),35 quoted by Parker Palmer: *A Hidden Wholeness: The Journey Toward an Undivided Life* (San Francisco: Jossey Bass, 2004), 129.

30. Shirley MacLaine quote listed at quotefancy.com. Websearch 8.2.17.

31. George Sand quoted in *Each Day a New Beginning*, Hazelden Meditation Series (Harper/Hazelden, 1982), December 2.

32. Dawna Markova, *I Will Not Die an Unlived Life* (Boston, MA: Red Wheel/Weiser, 2000), 17.

33. Fannie Flagg, *The Whole Town's Talking* (New York: Random House, 2016), 273.

34. Helen Mallicott, *Listen for the Lord* (Kansas City: Hallmark, 1977), 2, quoted in Linda Douty, *How Can I Let Go If I Don't Know I'm Holding On?* (Harrisburg: Morehouse Publishing, 2005), 90.

35. Kate Braestrup, "I'm Not Invisible," *Woman's Day*, Dec. 2014.

36. R. Jack Hansen and Jerry Haas, *Shaping a Life of Significance for Retirement* (Nashville: Upper Room Books, 2010), 62.

37. Psalm 90:12 *NRSV, New Revised Standard Version of the Bible*, copyright 1989 by the Division of Christian Education of the National Council of Churches of Christ in the United States of America. Used by Permission. All rights reserved.

38. Debbie Ford, *The Secret Shadow: The Power of Owning Your Whole Story* (San Francisco: Harper, 2002), 83, quoted in Rochelle Melander, *A Generous Presence: Spiritual Leadership and the Art of Coaching* (Herndon, VA: The Alban Institute, 2006), 250

39. Judith Ann Parsons, *The Clear and Simple Way* (Orlando FL: Dandelion Enterprises, 2004), 67 quoted in Linda Douty, *How Can I Let Go If I Don't Know I'm Holding On?* (Harrisburg: Morehouse Publishing, 2005), 56.

40. Mark Nepo, "The One Life We're Given: Finding the Wisdom That Waits in Your Heart," *Spirituality and Health*, July/August 2016.

41. John Maynard Keyes (http://www.keepinspiring.me/quotes-about-creativity-imagination-and-innovation/3ixzz4oWDnmkwl, web search 7.31.17.

42. Psalm 143 NRSV, New Revised Standard Version of the Bible, copyright 1989 by the Division of Christian Education of the National Council of Churches of Christ in the United States of America. Used by Permission. All rights reserved.

Suggested Reading

Athill, Diana, *Alive, Alive Oh!*. New York and London: W.W. Norton and Company: New York and London, American Edition, 2016.

Beattie, Melody, *Stop Being Mean to Yourself, A Story about Finding the True Meaning of Self-Love*. San Francisco: HarperSanFrancisco, 1997.

Berg, Elizabeth. *The Pull of the Moon*. New York: Random House. 1996.

--------. *The Year of Pleasures*, New York: Random House, 2005.

Brokaw, Sarah. *Fortytude*. New York: Voice/Hyperion. 2011.

Chast, Roz. *Can't we talk about something more PLEASANT?*. New York: Bloomsbury, 2014.

Chittister, Joan. *The Gift of Years*. Katonah, NY: BlueBridge. 2008.

Das, Lama Surya. *Letting Go of the Person You Used to Be: Lessons on Change, Loss, and Spiritual Transformation*. New York: Broadway Books. 2003.

Davidson, Sara. *Leap!: What Will We Do with the Rest of Our Lives? Reflections from the Boomer Generation*. New York: Random House. 2007.

Douty, Linda. *How Can I Let Go If I Don't Know I'm Holding On?* Harrisburg, PA: Morehouse Publishing. 2005.

Each Day a New Beginning: Daily Meditations for Women. Harper/ Hazelden, 1982.

Gawande, Atul. *Being Mortal*. New York: Metropolitan Book/Henry Holt and Company. 2014.

Hansen, Mark Victor and Art Linkletter. *How to Make the Rest of Your Life the Best of Your Life*. Nashville: Nelson Books. 2006.

Gray, Ruth Howard. *Survival of the Spirit: My Detour Through a Retirement Home*. Atlanta: John Knox Press. 1985.

Hagerty, Barbara Bradley. *Life Reimagined: The Science, Art, and Opportunity of Midlife*. New York: Riverhead Books, Random House. 2016.

Halaas, Gwen Wagstrom. *Clergy, Retirement, and Wholeness: Looking forward to the third age.* Herndon, VA: The Alban Institute. 2005.

Hansen, R. Jack and Jerry Haas. *Shaping a Life of Significance for Retirement.* Nashville: Upper Room Books. 2010.

Hollis, James. *Finding Meaning in the Second Half of Life.* New York: Gotham Books. 2005.

Job, Reuben P. and Norman Shawchuck. *A Guide to Prayer for Ministers and Other Servants.* Nashville, TN: The Upper Room. 1983.

Kurtz, Ernest and Katherine Ketcham. *The Spirituality of Imperfection.* New York: Bantam, 1992.

Lindberg, Anne Morrow. *Gift from the Sea.* New York: Random House, 1955, 1975, 1983.

Markova, Dawna. *I Will Not Die an Unlived Life: Reclaiming Purpose and Passion.* Berkley, CA: Conari Press. 2000.

Melander, Rochelle. *A Generous Presence: Spiritual Leadership and the Art of Coaching.* Herndon, VA: The Alban Institute, 2006.

Morgan, Richard L.. *Settling In: My First Year in a Retirement Community.* Nashville: Upper Room Books. 2006.

Morley, Patrick. *Second Wind for the Second Half of Life.* Grand Rapids, MI: Zondervan Publishing House. 1999.

Nouwen, Henri J. M. and Walter J. Gaffney. *Aging: The Fulfillment of Life.* Garden City, NY: Image Books, a division of Doubleday & Company. 1974.

Nouwen, Henri. *Bread for the Journey, A Daybook of Wisdom and Faith.* San Francisco: HarperSanFrancisco, 1997.

Palmer, Parker. *A Hidden Wholeness: The Journey Toward an Undivided Life.* San Francisco: Jossey Bass. 2004.

------ *The Active Life; A Spirituality of Work, Creativity, and Caring.* San Francisco: Jossey-Bass, 1990.

Peck, Scott. *The Road Less Traveled and Beyond: Spiritual Growth in an Age of Anxiety.* New York: Simon and Schuster. 1997.

Pipher, Mary. *Another Country: Navigating the Emotional Terrain of Our Elders.* New York: Riverhead Books. 1999.

Price, Eugenia. *No Pat Answers*. Grand Rapids, MI: Zondervan Publishing House. 1972.

Price, Reynolds. *A Whole New Life: An Illness and a Healing*. New York: Atheneum. 1994.

Prather, Hugh. *The Little Book of Letting Go*. New York: MJF Books. 2000.

Remen, Rachel Naomi. *My Grandfather's Blessings: Stories of Strength, Refuge, and Belonging*. New York: Riverhead Books. 2000.

Riley, Reba. *Post-Traumatic Church Syndrome: A Memoir of Humor and Healing*. New York: Howard Books, an imprint of Simon and Schuster. 2015.

Rohr, Richard. *Falling Upward: A Spirituality for the Two Halves of Life*. San Francisco: Jossey- Bass. 2011.

Stafford, Tim. *As Our Years Increase: Loving, Caring, Preparing for Life Past 65*. Grand Rapids MI: Pyranee Books. 1989.

Taylor, Barbara Brown. *Learning to Walk in the Dark*. New York: HarperOne. 2014.

Theole, Sue Patton. *Freedoms After 50*. Berkley, CA: Conari Press, 1998.

Thibault, Jane Marie and Richard L. Morgan. *Pilgrimage into the Last Third of Life: 7 Gateways to Spiritual Growth*. Nashville: Upper Room Books. 2012.

Zitter, Jessica Nutik,MD. *Extreme Measures: Finding a Better Path to the End of Life*. New York: Avery, an imprint of Penguin Random House. 2017.

About the Author

BETH LINDSAY TEMPLETON, Founder and CEO of Our Eyes Were Opened, Inc. is a public speaker, Presbyterian minister, retreat leader, and writer. A graduate of Presbyterian College and Erskine Theological Seminary, she worked for many years at United Ministries, a non-profit in Greenville, South Carolina, where she interacted with both "the have-nots" and "the haves." Since 2007, she has focused on a ministry with "the haves" so they can enlarge their thinking about people who live in poverty in order to reduce judgment and increase compassion.

Beth works with congregations, schools, universities, medical facilities, women's groups, civic groups, and businesses in Greenville and around the country.

She and her husband have three married sons and five grandchildren.

www.oureyeswereopened.org
beth@oewo.org

Made in the USA
Lexington, KY
08 November 2019